Praise for
THE BELONGING PARADOX

In **The Belonging Paradox**, *Dr Otito Iwuchukwu draws on her deep academic expertise and lived experience as an expatriate navigating cross-cultural contexts, life stages, faith settings, career roles and geographic locations to offer powerful insights on belonging. With candor, passion, vulnerability and wisdom,* **The Belonging Paradox** *takes us on a journey that at its core explores what it means to be human in today's polarized world.*

—Sosunmolu Shoyinka, MD, MBA,
Author of *Understanding Mental Health*

THE BELONGING PARADOX

THE BELONGING PARADOX

HOW TO FULLY BELONG. NO MATTER WHO YOU ARE, WHAT YOU ARE OR WHERE YOU ARE

OTITO F. IWUCHUKWU, PhD

GEFC Press

Copyright

Copyright © 2025 Dr. Otito F Iwuchukwu.

All rights reserved. No part of this publication may be reproduced, stored in a retrieval system or transmitted in any form or by any means— for example, electronic, photocopy, recording— without the prior written permission of the publisher. The only exception is brief quotations in printed reviews.

Cover Design: Jose Pepitor
Text layout and Design: Get Fab Editorial and Communications

Library of Congress Cataloging-in-Publication data on file at the Library of Congress, Washington, DC.
ISBN 978-1-7364244-2-1
ISBN 1-73642442-4

Printed in the United States of America
Published by GEFC Press
Boonton, NJ

This is a work of creative nonfiction based on a combination of facts about the author's life and certain events. All events in this book are portrayed to the best of the author's memory. While the stories are true, certain names and identifying details have been changed to maintain anonymity and to protect the privacy of the people involved. The reader should therefore not consider this book anything other than a work of literature.

Neither the author nor the publisher assumes any responsibility or liability whatsoever on behalf of the consumer or reader of this material. Any perceived slight of any individual or organization is purely unintentional. Any named resources in this book are provided for informational purposes only and should not be used to replace the specialized training and professional judgment of a properly qualified professional.

To Child 1 and Child 2,

Your entrance into my life put me on the path of learning how to belong to myself.

Thank you for the gift of your youthful wisdom and wit.

CONTENTS

Author's Notes	xvii
Introduction	19
PART I BELONGING IN FAMILY	**25**
I Hate Him, (and You?)	27
Family First. And Fourth	30
A Flip Flop of Familial Belonging	32
The Multiple Sides of Belonging	35
The Nature and Nurture of Belonging	39
Belonging and Family Group Settings	42
Family Focus Groups and Findings	46
Family: Our Defense Against External Exclusion	49
After Offense, Comes Repair	52
Home is What We Make of It.	54
Belonging Corner Reflections	55
PART II BELONGING IN FRIENDSHIPS	**56**
Friendships. Do We Want Them or Need Them?	58
The Circle of Friendships. How Large is Yours?	60
Re-Considering Friendship and Closeness	61
Finding the Words. Shyness, Introversion and Friendship	64
Friendship Discrimination with Age	66
Young Adulting with Friends	68
A Trip Home and Back to College	70

A Young Adult Friendship Unravels	71
A Framing Lens on Family Belonging and Friendship	74
Fully Grown. Yet Looking to Belong	76
Bringing the Unconscious About Friendship Forward	78
Friendship and Life, Interrupted	80
A Pandemic and A Ghostly Vision of Friendship	83
A Connector Disconnected	85
Of Gap Years and Making Friends. Going All Out	89
Looking for Friends. Good Friends	93
Belonging Corner Reflections	97

PART III BELONGING AT WORK — 98

Young Adults Divide. Then Unite	100
The Glory of the Latter Days	102
An Intro to Class Acts in Graduate School	104
Lab Work Compatibility	109
Post-Graduation: A Cross-Country Move	111
Working Two Jobs. For the Bills, and Non-belonging	114
A Country Criss-Cross of Work Belonging Memories	117
A Warm Woman in Cold Work Climates.	123
Reflected Work Belonging States	126
On Being Considered a Diversity Number	129
Your Contributions Are Valued. True for Some but Not All	131
An Understanding of Workplace Belonging	133
On Non-Representation and Inclusion	135
A Leadership Change with Sidelining in Tow	138

A Career Distraction and Belonging States	143
Championing Differences and Found Not Wanting	149
Belonging Corner Reflections	153

PART IV BELONGING IN THE FAITH — 154

Faith Spaces as Liminal Spaces.	156
A Believer and The Church	158
Coming to Church in America	163
Church in the South	165
The Southern Winds of Church Community	167
Clear Air Turbulence	171
Flying Back East	177
Migrating North: Northeasterly Church Winds	178
Am I a True Jersey Christian Girl or Not?	180
Am I Invited to The Party?	189
Separate and Together in Church	191
The Small Groups: In-Groups and Out-Groups	194
Church Notes: Doing Belonging Well at All Levels	196
Belonging Corner Reflections	199

PART V BELONGING IN PARENTHOOD — 200

Diversity Across Generations	202
Going to School from Home	205
ADHD is Awesome. Or is It?	211
Of Neuro-Diverse Children (and Parent)	216
The Nurture Debts We Owe and Are Owed	218

Friendships and Parental Belonging: Different Worldviews   221
A Researcher-Parent and Educator's Notes   223
Belonging Corner Reflections   226

BELONGING: A BRIEF EXPLAINER, OR TWO   **227**

A WALK THROUGH THE PARADOX OF BELONGING   **236**

A Framework for Lived Belonging   **241**

Bringing Belonging Back to Yourself (and Others)   249

Fostering Belonging at Work   **268**

Organizational Belonging: Right and Not So Right Ways   270
Becoming Wise About Belonging: To Care is to Intervene   274
Ways to Enhance Organizational Belonging   277

Concluding Thoughts   **286**

ACKNOWLEDGMENTS   **288**

Postscript   290
Bookending Family Belonging: A Story and a Poem   291
An Immigrant-Citizen's Belonging Poem   303

Notes   **307**

Author's Notes

This is not a book for everyone, unlike what you may read in many books. Rather, I wrote this book for people like me. Those who walk around with a nagging feeling of wanting to belong fully in the spaces they occupy. Of knowing they should belong but still find it hard to enter into the fullness of that belonging. People for whom the fear of rejection is a hidden albatross hanging on their shoulders, pecking away at their belongingness.

*

"What's all this talk about belonging?" that pecking translated into the familiar voice inside your head might ask. But you know what all the talk is about. You know, because it is this fear of rejection and associated non-belonging that sometimes makes you take a step back instead of forward. It is the fear that makes you not send that email, makes you not speak up, makes you not ask when you should. And on and on it goes. And you know without a shadow of doubt that there has to be a better way. This book will provide a compassionate roadmap to that better way. In this book, we will take roads less traveled on a journey where we will need to go back in order to go forward. But when you and I return to the present, we will be much better equipped than we have ever been to navigate the future.

*

This is a book that has belonged in my heart for so long but I was too afraid to release it and share it with the world. The journey of this book is similar to the journey of me, and perhaps of you reading it wherever you are. Sending this work into the world where it should belong may not end up the in ways I presume. But that would be just fine too. As the author, I have learned and I am still on a learning journey. The journey of learning how to belong, no matter who, what or where. No matter who says I belong or do not belong. No matter what supposed places of belonging I find myself in, and no matter where those places are located.

*

I hope you will find this book a suitable companion on your own journey to true belonging.

Now, let's journey on.

INTRODUCTION

As someone born after 3 failed pregnancies —my mom's own rainbow babies— one could say from a chromosomal point of view that I was determined to belong from birth. Leaving any and all circumstances of birth aside, many of us it seems, exist day in and day out, in liminal spaces, experiencing spaces of deep belonging while simultaneously existing outside of an unspoken and unseen societal framework of belonging. And sometimes we get so tired of this in-between-ness, that all we want to do is just go 'home.'

Because there's no place like home? ...

When you hear the word belonging, what comes to mind? Take a minute and picture what belonging means to you. What does it feel like? How does it feel? In what places do you belong so thoroughly that you don't even have to think about it? When we think of spaces and places that make you go, "Belonging? What's that? Is there any other way to be?" For some of us, most of the time, it would probably feel like home.

Outside of home, many places and spaces in life would have you and me searching for the initial feelings we had when we crossed the unseen threshold leading into them. As one of the earliest examples of outside spaces, do you remember your first day in kindergarten (replace kindergarten with nursery if you were raised in a diaspora country like I was). For many of us, such memories may be too far away to access. This is good, because our brains cannot hold that much information in working memory. Another reason we may not remember is because most children at kindergarten age tend to have a "let's

INTRODUCTION

all be friends" worldview to life. Where such friends are not based on status or any of the other criteria that older kids and adults use to differentiate who should or should not be in their friend groups.

To answer one of my many questions on belonging; Any place or space where you don't have to think about belonging is one where you are most likely to fully belong. The real question is how do we access this place? My goal in this book is to help you find and return to that place, both mentally (head) and emotionally (heart). For many like me, finding and returning to this place may mean that we have to go back in order to go forward. And a good place for most of us to go back to would be to go back home.*

What Airbnb can teach us about homecoming

The ubiquitous travel and hospitality sharing app Airbnb proudly declares within its mission statement that the company exists "to create a world where anyone can belong anywhere"... this with an aim to foster both a sense of belonging, and a world where anyone can feel 'at home' anywhere.

I really like this statement, despite not ever having booked a stay at an Airbnb, for reasons both known and kept to me. Their mission statement appeals to me because it calls to mind the feeling of "coming home (homecoming) or of "being at home", with 'home' being the common denominator.

---

*A caveat here: This would generally apply only if you were raised in a home where you were deeply loved, and cared for, and where you experienced significant stability.

THE BELONGING PARADOX

A homecoming or a return back to the place where it all began for most of us will help identify the feelings, beliefs and attitudes that we can use to continue to fortify our sense of belonging. It can also be the place where we begin to sort out what went wrong and how we can get back to the essence of us before the break-up. A going back in order to go forward.

This book in its simplest form is about homecoming.

Coming home to yourself—a whole, fully functioning and flourishing self—in whatever season of life that self is in.

There is a deliberate flow in the exploration of belonging through the spectrum of human development in this book. From section 1 with its focus on our birth families through section 5 and its focus on the families we birth and nurture as parents (for those with children). Between these two bookends, are friendships (section 2), work (section 3) and faith or spirituality (section 4). At the end of each section are reflection questions to think through your own experiences or that of others in your life. The goal of these reflections, like the beam from a lighthouse is to shed some light on any hidden parts of key belonging experiences in your own journey.

I designed the various sections to reflect the different life areas that we humans need for a flourishing and meaningful life. These life areas, or what psychologists refer to as **life tasks**, include universal areas like love or intimacy, work, and friendships, and the not-so-universal ones, spirituality and parenting. You will notice that of all the different life areas covered in this book, love and intimacy in partnered relationships is not one of them as this area in my opinion deserves a separate book.

INTRODUCTION

How to read this book

Although this book tracks my (and others') belonging stories through various life stages and life areas, you do not have to read the sections as presented. If any of the life areas do not apply to you, feel free to skip them and go read the ones that apply as each section can be read as a stand-alone. And remember, you can always return to any of the sections as needed. The belonging framework I developed and present at the end, however, is for everyone — **No matter who you are, what you are, or where you are**. This after all is the premise of this book. That you and I can learn to fully belong to ourselves no matter where we are on the spectrum.

NO MATTER WHO, WHAT OR WHERE.

PART I

BELONGING IN FAMILY

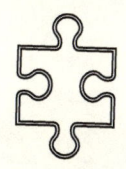

As humans we instinctively pay attention to whose belonging is being supported and whose is not in order to minimize damage from being subjected to the same things.

—Unattributed

If you are a parent of more than one child, you know this fact intuitively; each child is born different. In that light, could one say the same for belonging— Are we born with recognizing belonging? The same way some believe we were born with a quantifiable degree of our personality already formed. Are there intrinsic variances in the individual degrees of belonging and feeling the need to belong? How does the felt idea of belonging or non-belonging creep up on us? In the following pages, I explore belonging at the family group level from the strength of the attachment bonds we form with our parents, siblings, and other significant adults, to how we can repair belonging for our children after external onslaughts.

THE BELONGING PARADOX

I Hate Him, (and You?)

It was a relatively normal late afternoon in the summer of 2022. I picked up my sons from day camp and herded them to the car. On our way home, a raucous argument, as common with sibling brothers began. I tried, unsuccessfully, to concentrate on my driving and to stay out of their quarreling, having heard the older child (Child 1), say something that was both untrue and unkind to the younger one (Child 2). When Child 2 tried to refute the statement, Child 1 raised his voice several decibels higher in an attempt to drown out Child 2's voice and kept harping on what he had said earlier.

Now, as their momma, I must confess that this behavioral tic triggers me, not least because I think it is a bullying tactic often used by individuals who bully to intimidate and silence their targets. I asked Child 1, "Are you trying to drown out his voice so you can make him feel even worse, knowing that you said something terrible to him he was trying to defend himself?"

Before I could drive another few yards, the whole scene devolved, with tears and loud accusations being flung about how I loved Child 2 more than him. How I always took Child 2's side in everything. How Child 2 was my favorite, and how I did not love him, Child 1. He ended his tearful outburst by saying, "I wish I were the only child, and that Child 2 was never ever born." (Whoa! How did we just go from zero to one hundred? Talk about big emotions.) I replied, "That was an unfair accusation, and you know it" and continued the drive home. By the time we got home, he had calmed down and came to apologize to his brother and me.

As a child, he was done and gone, but the incident had me as his parent thinking for many days after. I thought about how he was completely clueless to the fact he had been an "only child" for 3 years and had been loved upon by us and his grandparents as one of the youngest grandchildren. I thought about how the accusation of favoritism had come full circle to haunt me despite all my striving not to replicate my own perceived feelings in my childhood home environment. Above all, I understood that this was his perceived reality, no matter how I tried to deny or refute it with mountains of evidence. He felt that I was playing favorites, and I had to live with the weight of that childish accusation, whether I liked it or not. I found myself thinking "I do not want to be the reason why this child will need therapy in his adult years, if at all." And most of all I thought, how on earth did I get here, to this full circle moment?

To understand the weight of this seemingly infantile rage-fueled accusation on my psyche, I would have to take you, across the Atlantic Ocean, all the way to Ikeja, the capital of Lagos, Nigeria, where I spent most of my childhood and adolescent years.

THE BELONGING PARADOX

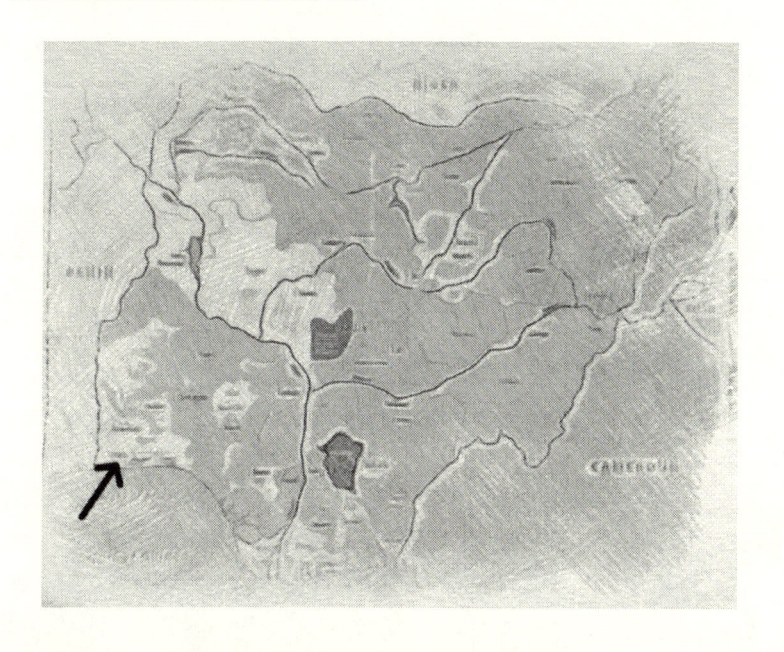

Outline of Nigeria (Arrow points to Lagos)

Family First. And Fourth

I grew up the youngest of four siblings. I love my siblings despite our inevitable differences, and I know they love me too. They may not understand me, what with my still being the talkative, action-oriented, sharpshooting last-born child that I was. But they accept me for who I am, and I know they are proud to call me sister. Much as I am to call them brother and sisters. While our parents raised us with little in material resources, they ensured we all got the opportunity of a stellar education. That you are reading this book is a testament to their sacrificial labor and love. Mom (bless her departed heart), a kindergarten teacher for 35 years, did her best to raise four children, while working and running a micro-enterprise, because teachers were paid so poorly at the time (and most are still underpaid).

As a child, maybe you never really knew the extent of your parents sacrifices in terms of how much money they had at their disposal to take care of you. I am not among that camp because I can still recall the shock I felt when I saw mom's paystub one day while rifling through her stuff (do not tell my Child 1 because I am now being subjected to the same invasion of privacy). I remember wondering if mom was a magician as I could not fathom how she managed to feed, clothe, and provide us, (and the constant stream of relatives that passed through our house) with other household necessities on such abysmally low pay.

Mom was quite the enigma, in retrospect. There is so much I could say, about my journey of trying to understand her. This, however, is not a book about my mom but rather about her

THE BELONGING PARADOX

daughter. Growing up, I observed what I considered a lot of mom-driven favoritism in our home. I do not think mom meant to favor her only son or the one daughter who was a spitting image of her. But that was what happened, by acts, whether of omission or commission. And being the youngest by a far stretch of age from the others, I was the quiet and sometimes not-so-quiet observer.

Mine was not a house where the youngest kid got spoiled, quite the opposite. The only place I would get some reprieve was while working on our family farm. I would go to work on the farm alright but my job as I saw it then was to keep the environment lively by talking off a storm while my sisters did their work and the parts of mine that would invariably be left undone since I spent the time talking. So much so, that I could not wait to go off to boarding school, because at least I would, in addition to boundaries around chores, have my own money, and my own goods. I would also not have to be forced to give up things for my older sibling or do my brother's laundry along with the myriad other responsibilities that fell on me as the youngest kid. The cumulative experience of growing up as the youngest child in my family and having to wait my turn for a few things, some of which never materialized, combined to produce an independent, somewhat willful child, with an entrenched sense of perceived fairness and justice.

This re-telling is not meant to be a "woe is me" one. Nor is it meant to be one of genetic determinism, which is the idea that I am who I am and what you see is what you get.[1] Rather, in my going back, it helps paint a personal background to bring forward the idea that who we become as adults, can be influenced by our environment, and by nature of our birth and birth orders in our families of origin. The unending nature vs. nurture debate.

A Flip Flop of Familial Belonging

Did I feel like I belonged in my family? I did and do still. I love my family very much. At the same time, when I remember some burning instances where I felt like mom displayed outright favoritism, I am still a bit chagrined. I used to think I should have gotten over this by now and get on with my life since we are now all adults who still love and respect each other.

As family stories go, I recently read a social question in The New York Times aptly filed under childhood confessions.[a] The question involved the case of a younger sibling who aided and abetted by their mother, stole her sister's clothes, over 50 years ago. This collusion, unbeknownst to the older one, who had worked part-time while in high school to earn money to buy her own clothes and had even learned to sew so she could make her own clothes. The husband of this older sibling was now, through this social question, recounting how she had discovered the 'betrayal'.

While the story itself did not bother me, the underlying tone of some mom-fueled favoritism caught my attention. Reading through the comments, I realized there are many adults who still feel the fresh pain from childhood events. The comments section (a gold mine for crowd pulse-taking) seemed evenly divided among the "Get over with it already, it was over 50 years for heaven's sake" versus "You can never understand the

---

[a] Philip Ganales "Why Did My Wife's Sister Confess to Taking Her Clothes 50 Years Later". *The New York Times*. June 12 2024. www.nytimes.com/2024/06/12/style/childhood-confessions.html.

pain of childhood betrayal and favoritism enabled by a matriarch." Phew!

I am certain that people in the former group would probably not be among those who would pick up this book to read. Because they may think certain expressed feelings are woo-woo and one ought to just get on with life, because what is past is past.

Is it though?

Why are some people invariably deeply affected by happenings in their past while others seem to breeze through life without a care in the world? It is almost like we were born with different thermostat settings for being able to tolerate degrees of remembering and re-experiencing. In the story I began this chapter with, I do not know if my older child would be deeply impacted by any continuing angst around belonging or non-belonging. He is a bona fide extrovert who gets his energy from people and is likely to go find a new group if he feels he is being excluded from some other group. This, in sharp contrast to his younger sibling who already shows signs of internalizing feelings of non-belonging. Feelings that I think he is made aware of in no uncertain terms at school, being a neurodivergent, gifted child with Attention Deficit/Hyperactivity and Social Communication Disorder (ADHD and SCD).

> **Q:**
> *How does the felt idea of belonging or non-belonging creep up on us?*

I see two variances at work here in my home. For my older son, the comparisons between his perceived sense of fairness about how he is treated in relation to his younger brother can spark either momentary or longer lasting feelings of not belonging at home. Yet, he can go to school and find his sense of belonging there among his peers and friends (I speak more about this in the section on belonging in friendships).

For my younger son on the other hand, because home is where he is accepted for who he is, where his neurodivergence is subsumed into our daily lives and is not made out to be a problem, he most likely loves being home, compared with being at school. Anecdotal evidence having shown us, on several occasions, that school is not his favorite place in the world. Such a child then, when at school, probably responds to anticipated social exclusion by keeping to themselves, which feeds into attendant feelings of non-belonging. This anticipation of social rejection can be a self-fulfilling prophecy leading to a self-reinforcing cycle of loner tendencies that can be hard to break out of. I know about this cycle because I have lived it. I lived it, and I can now write about how I am learning to live outside it as opposed to spinning inside it, like a harried hamster.

While the variances I speak above are extrapolated from my experience of my sons, you do not have to only take my word for it. Thankfully, there is plenty of research on belonging.

THE BELONGING PARADOX

The Multiple Sides of Belonging

The subjective feelings we associate with belonging does not mean it merely occurs as an innate, or personality driven feeling. As humans we interact with the society around us, agreeing or disagreeing with various societal structures, environments, and experiences. All of this provides us with a self-orientation that feeds into what we deem fair or right, acceptable or unacceptable. It also feeds into a sense of belonging or exclusion. Belonging can be facilitated or hindered by people existing within a defined social system (like our families) or within society through distinctions like class, gender, and group or ethnic affiliations. Despite how important then a sense of belonging is for a more satisfying life, people like me still have a hard time with it. I believe this has to do with a tendency to bunch all the concepts involved in belonging into one, as opposed to trying to examine its multiple sides.

◆◆◆◆◆

The recognition of belonging as a fundamental human need is no longer in question. Roy Baumeister and Mark Leary, two social psychologists, first made the case for our present taken-for-granted understanding.[2,3] Their definition of belonging as a core psychological need (or motivation) is what we see in polls and studies on the relationship between belonging and societal issues like loneliness and lack of civic engagement. There is, however, another category of belonging known as "state belongingness".[3] This state level belonging, where our feelings of belonging change according to how we evaluate our experiences with other people is comparable to other fluid human emotions like happiness and anger. This is because state belonging is influenced by the events and life stressors that we experience daily.[4] Depending on how frequent these encounters are, coupled with differences in individuals' perceptions (which may be based on personality), a person's subjective or state belonging can change multiple times a day.

Distinguishing between core and state belonging.

With state level belonging (and belongingness), one could go from general equanimity to feeling flustered and embarrassed over an incident at the checkout counter of a supermarket or bookstore, all because of how we emotionally appraised the encounter. The feeling of shame, anger, or disorientation that may overcome a person in such instances can be tied to subliminal questions like "Does a person like me not belong to this place?" Or "Is there something about me that led to the bad treatment I received, or am receiving?"

This subjective nature of state belonging is what makes communal conversations about belonging so hard. Different people by virtue of differences in personality traits (and learned behaviors) can have generally low or high levels of belonging that do not change much across time, and situations. Thus, in the example of the supermarket or bookstore incident, a person with lower levels of belonging will report a different experience from another with relatively higher state belonging.

THE BELONGING PARADOX

To test your intrinsic level of state belonging, think about the following scenario: A colleague passes by and flashes a smile. You might respond after thinking...

A. They like me and are happy to see me, or
B. Why do they have to put on that fake smile whenever they see me?

The thought and subsequent choice of option A or B will depend on many factors: your previous experience(s) with this individual, whether you think they are a genuinely friendly person, and even your culture.

As a rule of thumb, many culturally based interpretations convey a smile as a genuine sign of mutual affection. Some cultures, however, are more stoic and not very affective.[5] Thus, the colleague's smile may appear strange and make them out to be someone who cannot be trusted at first glance. Either way, the choice of A or B can determine your state level belonging in this encounter with a colleague.

> **Fun fact:**
>
> A smile is a big tell of body language, and humans it appears, are hardwired to read more into body language than actual spoken words. The concept of a fake smile or a non-Duchenne smile, and how to identify and differentiate it from a Duchenne or true smile was made popular by the work of emotion and deception researcher, Dr Paul Ekman, in *Lie to Me*[b], a popular 3-season TV series.[6,7]

[b] *Lie to Me*. TV Series 2009–2011. https://www.imdb.com/title/tt1235099/

The choice of B can be due to personality (a paranoid person due to low emotional stability) or can be based on low state belonging. Studies have shown that people who are socially excluded or rejected are better able to detect fake smiles. This adaptive response, likely developed to prevent wasted energy from attempting to foster relationships and affiliations with seemingly low chances of reciprocation, is common in people with lower levels of state belonging.[8] In short, these folks are like super detectors of fake friends through being more attuned to social cues of perceived belonging.[9] Smile for the camera, or for a friend, anyone?

> *Q:*
> ***What confers this varying sense of belonging on different individuals?***

This question cannot be answered adequately without taking a few steps back into the age-old question of nature and nurture. There is an age-old question regarding whether leaders are born or made. We can also frame this question in terms of belonging. And a reasonable answer will be that both options can be true at once.

THE BELONGING PARADOX

The Nature and Nurture of Belonging

Depending on who is doing the describing, belonging has been said to be a human motivation, a human need or a trait.[2,3] And like all other human drivers before it, some individuals are going to be more motivated than most others. If we consider belonging to be a fundamental need, as humans we have to satisfy this need in some way, in order to avoid a vacuum of need. Satisfying belonging needs will require spaces and places to belong, places where we can be ourselves, our natural 'homes' as it were. For some individuals, such places do not have to be big or broad. While others want to have it all. Individuals in the former category are those for whom the many questions of belonging about location, social connections, relational values, and fit, would not make any impressions. These are the ones when offering conscious responses to questions of fitting in, would always respond in the affirmative.

✦✦✦✦✦

The "nurture" or environmental aspect to belonging has to do with the kinds of environments and experiences that people are exposed to. Children for example who have experienced trauma as a consequence of adverse childhood experiences (ACE) such as growing up in poverty, being molested, or being exposed to domestic violence, tend to grow up as adults with an impaired sense of belonging.[10]

Although I began this book by talking about belonging being somewhat synonymous with the feeling of home, this is generally not true for home environments where adverse childhood experiences occurred. In such cases, home as a place and space of ideal belonging becomes non-existent. As a result, children raised in these environments experience what psychologists refer to as **belonging uncertainty**; persistent doubts about being accepted and fully belonging in the world.[11] Which is to say, home as a place where children can fully belong can no longer be counted on. As these children grow, it becomes harder to know who to turn to, where to turn to, and how to integrate into spaces and experience full belonging. I know this because I was such a child.

To cope with belonging uncertainty, some children develop different identities (being a class clown, a helper, or a risk-taker) to help them make sense of their experiences and help them meet basic psychological needs, including belonging.[12] For children with belonging uncertainty, leaning into one or more of these identities to avoid the shame from insecure state levels of belonging can hinder or help their need for secure relationships. This subsequently feeds into a lower (or higher) sense of belonging, much like adaptation gone wrong (or right).

Speaking of such adaptive behaviors attunes me to see the reverse, that even a child like my Child 2 who belongs fully at home, but who may feel like he has no friends, still has a high need for belonging. He may have adopted a loner identity as a coping mechanism to help him ward off unpleasant feelings that arise from others not accepting him for who he is.

THE BELONGING PARADOX

On Not Belonging in Your Own Family

The paternal side of my family has a very distinct culture of its own. I would say it's a bit more like a cult, in fact. Very group-think. If you don't completely sublimate your own wishes and interests to those of the group, then they treat you as an outcast. I could tell so many stories about this, but one very recent instance was that the "in" members of the family decided to go on a cruise. They put together a group of all the "in" 25 or 30 family members, including one or two of their friends and girlfriends/boyfriends. The age range was from 70 down to 8. My brother, who is "in", reached out to me and asked if I would like to go. I said thank you, but it wasn't really my thing. (A cruise is not something I want to go on, and furthermore, not with that group, as their values are quite the opposite of mine.) After the cruise, my brother at first told me all sorts of glowing stories about the experience. It took a couple of days for him to reveal the reality, that they had a very mixed experience, both because of the cruise and the family group. So, while I was glad I had learned to follow my instincts and not go, because I would have been miserable and felt like a complete outsider with this group, I was sad that I had to make that choice. But I will keep making the choice to stay safe, even though it hurts to be an outcast in your own family just because you have your own way of being.

~ JP

Belonging and Family Group Settings

It was Fall of 2020—The year a global pandemic wreaked havoc in our lives and forced many of us into forced home confinement. There I was, juggling student teaching and homeschooling my children, while attempting to maintain a modicum of composure through it all.

One chilly evening, amid all this, I heard a ruckus. I initially paid the boys no mind since random noises can be general background sounds in our household, until I heard Child 2 crying bitterly. His typical theatrics paled in comparison to these racking, guttural sobs. I called out to him, and he shuffled over to my desk in the temporary space I was using as a home-office. I asked what the matter was, and his next words to me were a question, "Mom, am I not important?" I turned fully toward him and asked, "What? Why? You're important, my love." "What's going on?" "What happened?" He pointed toward his brother and replied, tearfully, "Child 1 said I wasn't important and that nobody cared about me." My fragile mom-heart splintered into a thousand little pieces as I thought, "How can I show this child in this moment that he is important just as he is?"

This sibling-based discord between my boys reminded me again of the importance of words spoken over us, because as kids, we probably heard "Sticks and stones may break my bones, but words can't hurt me." As adults though, we know this to be false. Which is interesting because with my Child 2, I can think about how resilient children are and perhaps count on him not to remember this incident in the future. Yet, here I am, almost five years later, the whole scenario playing back vividly in my thoughts for an incident where I was a third-party mediator and not the direct recipient of these hurtful words. I remember asking Child 1 at the time, "How do you tell someone they're not important?" "How would you feel if somebody said that to you?"

◆◆◆◆◆

In many group settings, this consciousness of being or feeling unimportant can happen with us too, even as adults. We sense from others' actions and inactions that they do not deem us or our presence important but because we do not want to appear childish, we grin and bear it because as adult men and women, we don't cry right? Wrong!

But wait, why the talk about **group**s in a conversation on belonging in family settings?

> **A family is a group level unit of society.**

Work in the field of group dynamics provides us with a nice composite definition of this term—*A group is made of two or more individuals, connected by, and within social relationships.*[13] So, a family is a type of group, not only due to genetic inheritance but also because of the social and emotional relationships that tie its members together. A family (for those raised in one) is typically the first form of groups that we are socialized into. As a result, our experiences within this foundational group can influence how we interact with other groups in society, and our sense of belonging in these groups.

To be one of many children within a family is to be a member of a sibling group—a subgroup within a family group. The social and emotional identification aspects of groups may be one reason why siblings, although members of the larger family group may not readily identify with each other as a sibling group. Thus, we might hear statements such as, "We are siblings but we are not close." The word 'close' there and all it signifies is what makes for rich sibling group dynamics.

✦✦✦✦✦

As one of four siblings, I had a rich sibling group dynamic (at least between my sisters and me). Yet within our larger family group, I sometimes experienced feelings of disconnect because of the overall group dynamics facilitated by our more dominant group leader, who happened to be our mom, the tough matriarch. The identity that came out of this experience was one of unexplainable aversion (at the time) to groups and group-oriented activities. To be in a group was to ruminate about ill-conceived feelings of wondering when, or if, it would be my turn. It also meant having to wait 'to be picked' and to sometimes not get a coveted turn to participate. All, because home had taught me to wait, as a youngest child with older siblings who without fail, always got turns before I did.

As identity-bred interactions with life go, this aversion to groups led to generally avoiding group-related activities. Knowing that I tended toward independent thinking, I would sometimes avoid group settings. This avoidance further fueled my independent streak and became a type of self-fulfilling prophecy, since when you are in a group, you are supposed to do group things.

THE BELONGING PARADOX

People in tightly knit groups do not always take kindly to independence of thought (and any perceived disruption of stable group dynamics). As an independent thinker in such settings, you may find yourself directly or indirectly ostracized from the group, which further feeds into feelings of non-belonging. When I did find myself in social groups (which happened frequently, seeing as I am no hermit), and spoke out, sometimes against the group's cohesive thinking, I would invariably find myself singled out or left separate. In short excluded, while still in place.

Family Focus Groups and Findings

Since exploring the universality of belonging in life spaces was one of my stated aims for this book, I took the question of belonging beyond my family and ran focus groups. I spoke with mothers who had raised teen-aged to adult children. In these groups, I asked three questions:

1. Have you or your child ever been left out of a group?
2. How did it make you feel?
3. What did you learn from it and what would you tell your child or your younger self?

*"My whole family has **been left out** of our local homeschool community for over a year now and we have **survived the experience**. When we first moved into the community to begin our homeschooling journey, I made friends with some of the homeschool moms in my area, my kids made friends with their kids, we did everything together. I was feeling welcomed and loved, feeling like I belonged. Then everything changed when one of the moms feeling threatened by my presence, started spreading false stories about me and **stabbing me in the back**. Since we live in a tiny town, I could not avoid running into her, so I decided to ignore her when we attended events together so she would know her actions were not alright with me, and I no longer wanted to be friends. She retaliated by asking most of the other moms to choose between her and me. Since I was the newcomer, most of them chose her and stopped talking to me. The **group then started excluding our family** from all the homeschooling events*

THE BELONGING PARADOX

> *they were having. My kids were **devastated** to no longer be able to be with their friends. We survived by going out into town and creating more community in our lives. I will never again just have one major group of friends. I made sure to have both my kids find several other activities and groups to be involved in. Now if we ever get excluded again from one group, **it won't break our hearts**. We can now belong to another group or more to **carry us through the pain and hurt**. My oldest kid has learned that true friendship means standing up for your friends when you know they are being wronged. He's hurt but has learned a valuable lesson about who to consider a true friend. I told my children that sometimes people **will try to harm you on purpose** for no reason, but it doesn't mean you are not worthy of good friends. This particular group of homeschooling moms have shown that they don't deserve our family's friendship. And no one can break us or bring us down."*
>
> *~Mora*

Of the many responses I received, I was particularly moved by Mora's story. Not only because the experience she described happened in a homeschooling community, but also because of the sharp descriptions of this experience. Mora kept using the present form to describe the pain and the corresponding aftermath of this long past incident.

♦♦♦♦♦

Being excluded literally hurts. Moreso when the exclusion occurs in non-mainstream groups like Mora's homeschooling community where members consider themselves part of a joint cause and thus expect deeper social and emotional ties with each other. You can sense Mora's hurt in her story about her family's experience. The pain from experiences of exclusion or rejection is not limited to the past, neither is it a phantom one. Researchers have studied the connection between the pain from exclusion and physical pain and found similarities in how our brains process both types of pain.

Feelings of rejection and non-belonging are primal and uncomfortable, which is why most people avoid being the ones excluded from the group if they can help it, even if it means going against their beliefs and values. This may also be why people tend to avoid those who are being excluded or ostracized, lest they catch the social bug and become ostracized too, as we saw with the other moms in Mora's story. In other instances, it is the excluded individuals who withdraw from group members and avoid future relational interactions. Whatever form it takes, this sequela perpetuates the feelings of loneliness in the excluded persons. Thankfully, not with Mora, who realized the importance of community and proceeded to fortify her family's defenses against future episodes of non-belonging based on membership in a single group.

I say good for Mora because she found some of the ways to build back belonging for herself and her family, (ways covered in-depth in this book), even if she had to do it under initially stressful conditions.

THE BELONGING PARADOX

Family: Our Defense Against External Exclusion

I began this section on belonging in childhood in a family group setting and the importance of a supportive home base for helping children build their sense of belonging in the world. I witnessed a prime example of strong familial-level support and advocacy in the case of an eight-year-old Black gymnast who was overlooked during a medal ceremony.[c] This is a story I think about often. Due to the power of social media, I sometimes think this story was seen and heard around the world. But I also realize it could be a biased amplification of certain news for those in the Western hemisphere, and it was not such a huge story.

In the video snippet, a young girl, the sole Black gymnast on the team, was skipped by a white lady handing out medals to all contestants.[14] This faux pas was caught on camera, which was the reason I, and many others, witnessed this upsetting incident. What was so baffling (to me) was seeing the medal presenter with a solitary medal left on the tray after presenting to the last gymnast at the end of the line. And it never occurred to her to look back to see if every participant received a medal. The other aspect of this story that so many viewers commented on was about what I considered a type of **bystander effect**; how none of the adults there (especially the

---

[c] Joe Hernandez. 2023. *Irish gymnastics group apologizes after a Black girl was skipped at a medal ceremony.* September 26. NPR.
https://www.npr.org/2023/09/26/1201781803/black-irish-gymnast-skipped-snubbed-medal-apology.

event photographer taking pictures of each child being awarded a medal), intervened to make the presenter aware that she had missed a participant.[15] The subsequent scene where the gymnast's fellow team members rallied around to apparently comfort her, was both heart-wrenching and - warming all at once. This whole event. as seen on video, was a public show of non-belonging, and of what can happen when people do not speak up in the face of blatant exclusionary behaviors.

After the video made the rounds, the organization in question issued a statement declaring that the issue had been resolved; the participant had received her medal before leaving the field of play, and the official in question had resigned. This statement was an example of the equivocal responses that organizations tend to give in morally awkward situations. But the story was not quite over.

The family of the girl in question in a media interview following, denied some of these assertions stating that the organization never took full responsibility, or issued a public apology for the incident.[d] The mother also went on record to state that their family had experienced an ongoing pattern of subtle and non-subtle acts of exclusion, being the only Black family at gymnastics events hosted by this organization. The gymnast's mother asked for the organization to ensure the video was taken down so as to prevent their family from being subjected to any racist backlash. She also asked the organization to issue a full public apology.

---

[d] Mark Tighe. *Family of girl snubbed at medal ceremony want public apology from Gymnastics Ireland.* September 23, 2023.Irish Independent. https://www.independent.ie/irish-news/family-of-girl-snubbed-at-medal-ceremony-want-public-apology-from-gymnastics-ireland/a726462541.html

THE BELONGING PARADOX

Her advocacy paid off. Supporters of the family shared the video with Simone Biles, the four-time Olympic gold gymnast, who sent the young gymnast a personal message expressing support and encouragement.[e] The organization eventually issued a full *mea culpa*. They took responsibility for the official's actions at the medal ceremony, and committed to do better by the gymnast and others like her in the future.

---

[e] Mary Whitfill Roeloffs. *Gymnastics Ireland Apologizes For Snubbing Black Athlete— What We Know About The Incident Simone Biles Says 'Broke My Heart'*. September 25, 2023,. www.forbes.com/sites/maryroeloffs/2023/09/25/gymnastics-ireland-apologizes-for-snubbing-black-athlete-what-we-know-about-the-incident-simone-biles-says-broke-my-heart/.

After Offense, Comes Repair

As children, if we were wounded outside, knowing that we could always come back home, and people at home would take up arms and fight for us just like the gymnast's mother did, helps us see that the actions of adults (women or men) who should have known better did not have to define us for good. As an adult reading this book, please recognize how crucially important it is for children to see their families, or any of the adults in their lives advocating for them. Psychologists have shown that between the ages of eight and nine is when self-esteem begins to manifest in children.[16] The flavor of self-esteem at that age is usually linked to setting and achieving goals, as in the case of our little gymnast competing with her peers. While the little girl may remember the actions of the official, with regards to self-esteem, she is more likely to remember the actions of her family and the good words of Simone Biles. And this is how repair happens. It may be instant, or it may be over time. But repair can and does happen under the right conditions.

◆◆◆◆◆

As adults, one of the ways we can help the children in our lives with belonging is to ensure that we are creating environments of unconditional positive regard and acceptance. When it comes to belonging needs, two suggested remedies out of many, to mitigate the effects of traumas (big or small) from adverse childhood experiences in children involve: a) ensuring and supporting their sense of safety and b) encouraging a sense

THE BELONGING PARADOX

of belonging and connection.[10] In encouraging a sense of belonging and connection, caregivers, whether parents or not, must promote and practice unequivocal acceptance. They should recognize that the feelings of acceptance that follows belonging is a vital need for everyone, including those children, who because of traumatic experiences may have a higher need for belonging.[10] The key word here is *'may'*. Because we do not know how each child will respond to what experience, children need to see their parents and caregivers advocating for them. This helps assures them of their place in the world, starting from home.

Q:

If home has not been the best experience for you, how, and where, can you best find your home?

Home is What We Make of It.

Although I am all grown now, I am still my mother's daughter. I have had to, and I am still working through what it means to belong. Maya Angelou in her now immortalized words, reminds me (and you) that the price of finding true belonging is high, but the reward is great. I do this work so that my children can see me and know that belonging is their birthright. I do it so they can know that they belong everywhere and nowhere. It is my hope that anyone tracing their family lineage through past and present can take the stories here and the belonging framework built out of my work and life, with its heritage, history, and interwoven selves—Black woman, immigrant, mother, wife, daughter, sister, aunty, educator, scientist, social scientist, and woman of faith—and use it to build back their own sense of belonging. And in doing so, learn to be at home with themselves and others.

Belonging Corner Reflections

1) Did you feel a sense of belonging growing up in your household?
2) In what, if any, ways did your birth order impact your sense of belonging in the family system you grew up in?
3) How do you think your familial sense of belonging impacts your state belonging in the spaces you occupy in the world now?
4) "Am I not important?" A child asked me this pithy question. Have you ever felt a sense of this question in any of the spaces you find yourself? How did you respond to this question to your 'inner child'?" Are you satisfied with your answers? How can you become important to yourself, no matter who, what or where?

PART II

BELONGING IN FRIENDSHIPS

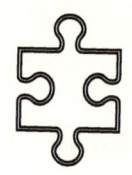

Friendship is never established as an understood relation. It is a miracle which requires constant proofs. It is an exercise of the purest imagination and of the rarest faith.

—Henry David Thoreau

Ah! Friendship. The hard-to-describe-but-easy-to-know-if-you are-in-a-good-one phenomenon. We all know what a good friend feels like. I use the word feel because when you are with a person you know in your heart is a good friend, you feel like you are with yourself. Good friends reflect the essence of who we are and who we consider ourselves to be. It has been said that a friend is a person with whom we can be ourselves. A person who knows us as we are, accepts us, supports us in good and bad times, and increases our ability to reciprocate the love and affection they show us. If that is not finding belonging with someone, then I do not know what is. Little wonder then why so many find it hard to make and be good friends. It is literally labor. A labor of love. Good labor: labor that offers us manifold rewards in terms of wellbeing.

Friendships. Do We Want Them or Need Them?

A friend is someone who sees you as you are and still likes you. Or in another definition attributed to Elbert Hubbard, "A friend is a person who knows all about you and still likes you."[1] To reflect about this touching definition in the reverse; "If someone we consider a friend no longer wants to be friends, does this mean that they see us, know all about us, and no longer like us?" Thinking about it in these stark terms can be distressing. Which is why the sting of perceived rejection from friendships gone awry without any identifiable explanation is one of a different kind.

With family groups, we think about the fact that we did not choose to be born into our family of origin. With friends (and friendships) however, choice is everything; we choose our friends (and they choose us). This voluntary choice is one that comes with unspoken loyalty bonds, along with the mutual feelings of affection, kindness, and goodness that one generally expects from friendships. Friendships are good for us; Good friends can make life more meaningful.[2]

♦♦♦♦♦

When it comes to wanting or needing friends, some it seems, are not in lack. These are the ones who appear to have a friend in every corner of the room, and world. Some of these people we may recognize as the butterfly (social butterfly) in terms of how frequently they seem to be in touch with so many people/friends.[3] Those with extroverted personalities fit readily into this description. We all know these people and may have some of them as friends, and even spouses. You may even be that person in your friend group. If you identify as a social butterfly, I say well done to you for your ability to keep your social connections going. Everyone needs someone like you in their friend circle.

The Circle of Friendships. How Large is Yours?

In writing this section, I thought, a lot, about the concept of Dunbar's number.[4] If you have never heard of this term, it was coined based off the work of Robin Dunbar, a British anthropologist. From his research in primate populations, Dunbar concluded (and still maintains) that humans have the mental capacity to maintain a close social group of 150 people at maximum.[a] He recognized, of course, that the quality of relationships with these 150 people cannot be the same. I emphasize this idea, just like Dunbar, with an illustration of friendship levels as concentric circles, with close friends at the center.

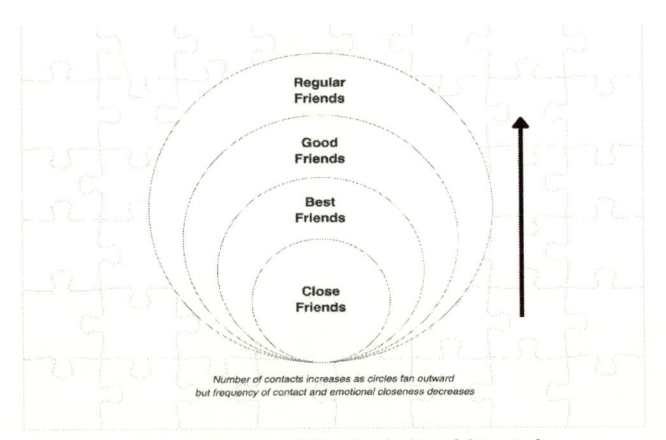

My conception of Dunbar's friendship circles

---

[a] A personal note about Dunbar's research; By all accounts, I do not believe that the number of people in my friendship circles come close to his famed number.

THE BELONGING PARADOX

Re-Considering Friendship and Closeness

I have nothing against Dunbar and his research. In fact, I learned a lot from reading his seminal work on friendship while doing research on this chapter. But from a personal point of view and experience on belonging, I want to tease apart what we mean when we say close friends. This, being in my experience, the difference between what we consider quality friendships and how such friendships play out in life. Before going on, I must confess that I am one who has been guilty of seeing things from a binary perspective when it comes to relationships. A friend was either there or not, there was no in-between. This meant that I viewed friendship the same way too for many years. If a person was my friend, then the mutuality had to be reciprocal, or I could not call you a friend.

I have had to use cognitive behavioral techniques to sort through the effects of such binary thinking. This is not to say that I have lowered my standards of reciprocity in relationships, I am simply wiser about how to expend mental capacity and limited time and resources —all things that have to be used in attempts to make and keep friends.

Who Makes a Close Friend?

Is it someone you have been together with since kindergarten, who lives ten houses down from you, in the cul-de-sac where you played every day after school? Is it someone who can show up unannounced at your doorstep and you would be all too happy to let them in and make them a bed and a cup of hot cocoa? The answer is going to depend on time and circumstance and location.

For some, the kindergarten friend would be considered a best friend forever while another would consider that same kindergarten friend, a good friend. In my world, I used to define a close friend as someone who you can call at any time and you can catch up right where you left off, without feeling like any time had passed. They knew you; you knew them. You were comfortable telling them your secrets and not-so-secrets and they would not bat an eyelid. Your relationship was not bound by time and distance.

✦✦✦✦✦

For other types of friendships, distance unintentionally becomes the barrier to their maintenance. With these types, you became friends due to proximity. Once either party moves away, the friendship moves away too, as I like to say, gradually fading over time to little more than a few texts or few and (really) far-between phone calls. Social media has not helped with these kinds of friendships because it offers the illusion that you are in touch since they like and comment on your posts. But, when you apply the social media criteria for friends into a much smaller and proximal circle, it fails the test.

Then, you have the other kind of friends who enter, as it were, into your best or good friend circle, showing up for every event, having sleepovers with kids (where both parties have kids), and going on joint family vacations. But gradually, then suddenly, you find yourself outside their regular friend circles. And you know this because you see them with new close

THE BELONGING PARADOX

friends, who in some cases, you connected them to in a bid to enlarge your mutual friendship circles.

So many layers. And so many ways to deconstruct these layers of closeness in friendships depending on who you ask. Yet again, as much as I know that personality cannot and does not explain everything, I cannot speak on friendship and belonging without reference to this important aspect of self.

Finding the Words. Shyness, Introversion and Friendship

When I hear people speak of kindergarten friends, I smile. If only, because I have no recollection of kindergarten or nursery school, as we called it back home. I vaguely remember following mom to school and being dropped off in some vacuous space of a classroom, which was nothing like I had imagined school to be. For someone who had cried every day to be allowed to follow my siblings to school, nothing prepared me for the actual experience. My parents packing up and moving 600 miles away and my starting elementary school in a different part of the country did not help with childhood memory storage and retrieval.

Even in elementary school, where I was a 'popular' kid because I was always top of the class, I do not recall many friends from that era. I only recollect three friends, because I happened to attend the same high school as one of them and briefly reconnected with the other two in college. It was only in middle school (junior secondary school) that I started to come into my own with friends and friendship. Although I was an incredibly chatty child at home, I could hardly find the words outside when in the company of persons I either did not know or was not comfortable with. I had developed an internalized severe stranger-danger outlook after an adverse childhood experience.

This, and coupled with the fact that I went to boarding school for middle and high school where social comparison was a sport, quickly alerted me to the fact that people affiliated

THE BELONGING PARADOX

with others for status gains. I did not make friends easily because I used to be what I called then a shy person. It was only with age and understanding, I came to understand it was not really shyness or social anxiety at all but rather introversion. I do friendships really well in small circles, but any larger and I freeze, with the attendant consequences of being called aloof or distant. The bane of many introverted people.

Friendship Discrimination with Age

For someone already used to living in her head through reading and daydreaming, I did not consider having few friends an issue. Boarding school entailed we were always in groups whether for assigned duties, for classes, for afternoon or evening preps (what we called homework and reading sessions). I did not notice a dearth of friendships because there was not much room to make them at the beginning.

As I got older, in high school, I started to be more discriminating about friendships. I knew who I liked and did not like. I also knew who liked me and who did not. I had no mortal enemies as far as I remember. I only remember getting the occasional snide comments from a few of the girls about how amazed and "jealous" they were at how easily schoolwork came to me. But it was not something I feared I would be undermined for.

I, on the other hand, had many friends that I always wished my parents were as rich as theirs. I remember visiting their beautiful homes and wondering if we would still remain friends, should they have ever visited me in return, since for some reason these visits were always one-sided. In retrospect, I look back now and wonder if I created the conditions for non-reciprocity by asking them not to bother visiting and I would do the visiting. Or if it was a case of not being proximal enough for them to count it as a friendship's obligation. I would never know.

And being that for some of these high school friends, our friendships have survived over decades—through parent and

THE BELONGING PARADOX

sibling loss, marriages and non-marriages, then I guess it does not really matter in the end. This to me is the beauty of the friendships we make in adolescence, when they do last, they are true survivor friendships, having weathered so much in-between.

> *I was fresh out of high school and wanted to connect with my peers, who had no connections with school. I had felt like an outsider for the most part of high school, you see. To provide more context, I had attended a girls only boarding school.*
>
> *A friend from high school invited me to a youth fellowship in town. From the moment I stepped in I felt a sense of belonging. Both boys and girls were welcoming, no airs, no hint of "class-system".*
>
> *What I learned from that experience is that people remember how you make them feel. I want the world to be more open to include people who don't dress like them or talk like them or are not from their socioeconomic background.*
>
> *~ SA*

Young Adulting with Friends

Getting into the college of your dreams is always such a pinnacle of goal attainment for a teenager fresh out of high school. To attend said college and then make life-long friends (or so it seemed then, because time does tell), was sweet icing on the cake. This was my story, going off to college in 1994 in Southwestern Nigeria.

In my first week as a college freshie, I caught up with a long-time family friend who had gained admission too. He introduced me to his newfound guardians. They had a daughter my age who promptly became a new best friend (or so it seemed, again). I also met a friend from high school who chose this college as her top choice. She chose this school as opposed to the one opposite our high school, which was where most of the girls from our secondary school typically went. What I forgot to mention was that I was not from any of those parts. I had picked a high school far from home to establish some independence. When it came to college, I picked a school far away from high school but now close enough to home that I could go home at will if I needed to on a whim. Life settled down pretty quickly and I would go on to expand my friendship circle, becoming friends with people who were also friends of my family friend. Are your eyes glazing over already at this crisscrossing of friend circles?

It was in these early adult years that I learned more about friendships than ever. I made so many mistakes in terms of either being too friendly or not being friendly enough, but as with all things I began to settle with a core group. Here, now, were friends who would come visit my home in whatever

THE BELONGING PARADOX

condition, and I would visit them in return, spending our holidays with reciprocal visits. In those days we had no phones, whether cell or home phones. We found our ways to one another's houses using mere descriptions like, "Get off at Cement Bus Stop. Walk down the road on your right, you'll see a big green house with a black gate opposite a hair dressing salon with a refrigerator in front of it. Just knock on the gate and we'll come let you in." If you are laughing as hard as I am while writing this, I would not blame you. It was a wonder we never fell prey to nefarious characters.

It was also in this young adulthood stage that I knew what it felt like to experience non-belonging based on what I considered exclusionary behavior. In retrospect, this experience shattered my naivete, opening my eyes to differences in values and personality based on nurture and how people navigate life in the presence of others. These are things I am still learning, fortunately (or unfortunately), depending on how you view it.

A Trip Home and Back to College

Recall that I now had a new 'best friend' through a connection with my family friend. This friend was a bona fide campus kid due to her dad being a staff at the university. This campus (my alma mater) having been built during the British colonial period, was gorgeous to say the least. Living and schooling (elementary to college) there was its own subculture for the staff kids. I got introduced to this new world through my friend and loved it. I admired the intellectual lifestyle and the access to social and relational capital they had as a result of being raised in the ivory tower.

My new friend and I became so tightly knit that we were quite the item even though she was in the humanities, and I was in the sciences, two different faculties, on different sides of the campus. This had no effect on our friendship as we managed to see each other quite frequently. We enjoyed one another's company and no matter the differences in our backgrounds, I thought we made a good team.

Some time in our third year of school, we had a national teacher strike, and we were asked to go home without a return date in sight. My friend asked if she could come home with me and I remember telling her I did not know if she was going to be comfortable coming to stay in my house, because I did not come from rich stock. She in turn said none of that mattered and that all she wanted was to go away with someone her parents trusted.

THE BELONGING PARADOX

A Young Adult Friendship Unravels

She did come home with me for a few weeks. We went about town, and I showed her some street savviness what with her never having traveled that far away from campus. The strike did end, and we all returned to school. One late evening after another lovely visit, as we walked back to their house, this time in company of her younger sister, they began teasing about a neighbor of theirs. Talking about how the neighbor was so full of themselves despite not having much in the way of material things. That this neighbor would always appear dapper, while living in a house that did not pass muster.

And it hit me, that bodily sensation of feeling hot and cold all at once, something I now realize was a prelude to anxiousness. My mind galloped with thoughts, ranging from "How could someone who had come to my own apparently threadbare home say such things in my presence?" "Did it mean they were also laughing about the state of my home when I was not with them?"

I bade my goodbyes that day and left in a restless state of mind. If I had a relationship trustometer, the temperature of our friendship must have fallen a few points that day. If only that were the end, I might have moved along but the trustometer temperature dipped even further the next year when I was asked by this same friend to defend the sanctity of my relationship with my boyfriend.

The second and third year of college was awash with romantic pairings (and courtships). We were not to be left out. Even with having a family house on campus, my friend who was now dating a handsome young man moved into the residence hall. I too had also began dating a boyfriend (now spouse) who became a good friend to my friend too. Once in a while, we would go hang out in my friend's house (because home was always better than campus housing).

One certain day as we lounged in the house, her mother returned from work and did not seem too pleased to see us waiting for the daughter to return from school. We did not know it then, but her mom, even though she knew each of us separately, did not want us (as a confirmed couple) alone in the house, because of appearances. So, when my friend came looking for me to tell me that her mom was not happy that I brought my boyfriend to the house, I was perplexed. "What changed?" I wondered. Was it the fact that her mom was now aware that we were dating that made us a girl and boy who could not be together alone in their house. Her mom had always known both of us as individuals and fondly called us her kids too.

✦✦✦✦✦

I remember asking my friend, "What was your mom worried about?" She said she did not know, and she was just relaying the message she had been asked to do. In this case, the second message she relayed was that her mom asked that we no longer visited their house again as a pair. To say that I was hurt would be the understatement of that decade of my life. Because here I was at 21 years old being told I was no longer welcome in their house, by same friend serving as a human telegraph. This incident marked the sudden demise of a friendship that had been slowly eroding due to what I perceived as our very different values around socioeconomic status.

THE BELONGING PARADOX

Again, one can only retrospectively reflect and realize that our home and family culture plays a huge role in our outlook on life (and friendships). Because as child raised to be very independent minded, my mom, also very conservative in her own ways, would probably not have brought up such an observation with me. And even if I was told to give a friend such an uncomfortable message, unless she, mom expressly asked for evidence, I would probably have skipped such a task (not great, I know!).

I cannot imagine, then or now, being in my friend's shoes, raised in an environment with an ultraconservative mother whose word was law. I did not have that experience, and I can only empathize now in retrospect, with many years in between. My friend probably never thought there was any other option or ways to soften the impact of the delivered message. After all, she was not me and therefore did not know how badly I would take it.

So many years later and this story is still a little hard to recount, because my interpretation and framing at the time negatively impacted my state belonging, and therefore my friendship with her and the family. It was not just the rejection itself that hurt, but also the meaning I ascribed to it. How we frame and make meaning of a belonging experience can hurt us even more than the actual encounter. (The section on Belonging Practices speaks more about how to reframe well).

A Framing Lens on Family Belonging and Friendship

If I must be honest about my feelings, which I always try to be but do not always succeed, I met my friend's family by proxy. She was the first friend made outside the confines of the social groupings at my all-girls boarding school. I was thrilled to be her friend, and a friend of the family.

On the parental side of her family, however, I always felt like a spare. For some reason, her parents bonded with my family friend's parents and not mine. In fact, my family friend became their adopted child because they hosted him in their house for months until he found his own accommodations and he came and went freely all through our college years. Something that did not happen with me. While my bonding and friendship with their daughter made up for it, when I got the message about her mom saying that she would prefer I not come to their house, it cut me way deeper than it should ever have. From my perceptual lens, it appeared like a repeat of choosing another child over me. This lens obviously colored everything else beyond that to the point where I felt like there was no point in being friends with the daughter again, if I could not be accepted by the mother.[*]

That whole incident and its aftermath birthed a seed in me. One of non-attachment to larger family bonds when making

---

[*] My friend and I did find each other in our adult years post graduations, weddings and babies. But the flavor of the relationship had changed with time, distance and variances in life orientations. Maturity had done its work and we are both the better for it (At least for me, otherwise I would not be writing about it).

THE BELONGING PARADOX

new friends. I learned to recognize that I could be friends with someone without necessarily being friends with their families. I learned to draw and lean into my respective boundaries when required. I have friends now that I am fully aware that their husbands could care less about our friendships, but it does not impact our relationship. This familial non-attachment mindset has kept many a friendship alive since. I show up when needed for my friend(s) and vice versa but I also keep my boundaries where their spouses are concerned, because I do not have or need to be friends with their spouses. Mutual respect from all parties involved was going to have to be enough.

Fully Grown. Yet Looking to Belong

One thing I can count for myself as an adult is having an interesting fortune with friendships. Good fortune too, if I were to go by my history of nomadic movement as a child and the lack of affiliations from my adolescent years. Those pivotal years when people formed their versions of themselves as popular or friendly, did not come easy for me.

College, however, paid me back in multiple doubloons. While I could still trace a finger to say that I never made strong affiliations with my classmates per se, I did make a core group of friends in another field. Folks who are still my friends to this day, twenty some years later. Many of these friendships now exist across time and space, as a lot of us happened to have emigrated either to North America (US and Canada) or to the United Kingdom, with some brave souls going further to Australasia. Many of us emigrated for higher education; MBAs, MPHs and PhDs, and yet others for work through foreign medical graduate pathways.

As a result, we bonded even more through years of relentless studying, working long hours and being severely underpaid, or even working for free. All this to get those coveted intern hours that would enable us obtain our professional licenses. We faced so many trials, rejections, and stories of malevolence from those in the societal majority. Still, we persisted. We met up with each other at key social events—weddings, our children's births and birthday parties, pastoral ordinations, landmark birthday parties and other celebratory events. Each face-to-face visit or meeting, and our incessant

THE BELONGING PARADOX

voice and video chats always left me thinking how blessed I was to be among these friends.

But… younger persons like my son reading this might ask, "Why must there always be a but?" To which I will say, "There does not have to be a but, if we are able have greater consciousness and awareness of life cycles" … When certain things in life are not being consciously and intentionally regenerated, then degeneration becomes a natural consequence of this inattention. So, too with friends, and friendships.

Bringing the Unconscious About Friendship Forward

Every one of us can probably tell what good friendship feels like and what we think are the qualities of a good friend. We all desire the enduring power of good, stable, and positive platonic friendships in our lives. For those of us who are Christians, even the Scriptures refer to *"a friend who sticks closer than a brother."*[b] It also goes without saying that friendships are critical to social health for us, because a good friend(s) will be there for us through the years, even when family is not.

Robin Dunbar, in his writing on social circles and friendships, lists what he called the seven pillars of enduring friendships—the similarities we see in people that makes it easy to bond with them. This phenomenon of instant clicking is referred to as homophily, the principle of similarity, or like attracting like. The seven pillars include: **having the same language (or dialect), being from the same place (or growing up in the same area), having similar educational and career trajectories, having similar hobbies and interests, having the same worldviews (whether religious, moral, or political), having similar musical tastes**, and **having a similar sense of humor**.[5]

The more of these pillars we have in common with another person, (same or different sex), the stronger the relationship we will have, and the friendlier and kinder we will be to one another. In fact, Dunbar refers to these pillars as 'signals of

---

[b] Proverbs 18:24, New King James Version © 1982 Thomas Nelson

THE BELONGING PARADOX

belonging' or cues that let us know that we belong with a group of people. With many of my college friends, having so many pillars in common across us all, made for enduring friendships that survived cross-country moves.

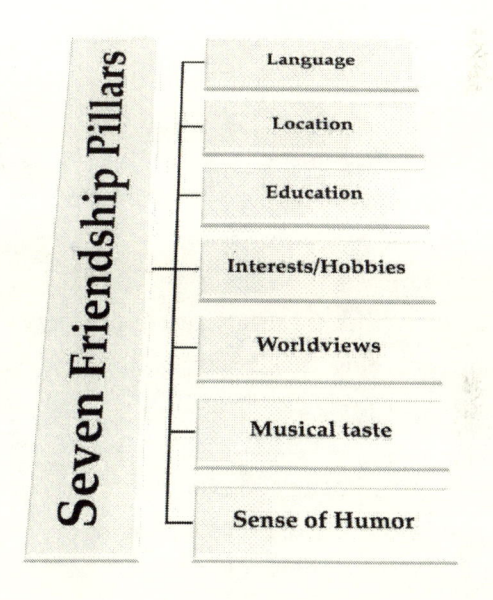

Seven Friendship Pillars
- Language
- Location
- Education
- Interests/Hobbies
- Worldviews
- Musical taste
- Sense of Humor

Sharing majority of these seven pillars with our friends makes for satisfying friendships

Friendship and Life, Interrupted

The pull of life's responsibilities; getting married, having children, building a career, takes its toll. And nowhere more than on our friendships. These voluntary associations in friendships, associations that are so vital to quality of life are, ironically, the ones we so readily leave adrift as we navigate our adulthood.[c]

It was no different with my college friends and me. We were all fortunate to have immigrated at about the same time and were able to support one another through it. But differences in immigration periods, and career paths (in terms of starting the climb up that proverbial career ladder), can exert a steep tax on friendship ties if we stand by and allow it. An impact that is seen with both same-sex and opposite-sex friendships. While some enduring friendships outlast distance, appearing like you easily pick up where you left off, in my experience, three things tend to have the greatest effect on the ongoing quality of adult friendships: proximity to your friends, getting married, and having children (or not).

When I came to the US, I knew that living in Philadelphia was going to be semi-temporary, so I never fully considered building a life there. Yet, while in graduate school, I recall seeing so many of my friends getting MBAs and other less time-consuming degrees and moving on to work in finance and wondering if I had made a mistake. The pain I felt on

---

[c] Julie Beck, "How Friendships Change in Adulthood." *The Atlantic*, October 22, 2015. www.theatlantic.com/health/archive/2015/10/how-friendships-change-over-time-in-adulthood/411466/.

THE BELONGING PARADOX

seeing friends move away as they finished programs, got jobs in far flung places across the country, and relocated on the daily, was visceral. I slowly began to realize how much I disliked endings, as necessary as they are/were. Each move to me felt like the end of a friendship. Even though we promised each other we would keep in touch, I also knew that nothing beat proximity for maintaining close relationships.

After relocations, came the marriages, and for some, parenthood. Most of my friends married long before me as I was in no hurry to tie any knots (for reasons beyond the scope of this book). But suffice to say, when it came to the marriage bell curve, among my friends, I was a lagger by at least 5 years. This meant that many of them also became parents well before I did. Going back to Dunbar's friendship pillars, two of the seven pillars were now like reeds, shaky at best, since I no longer shared these commonalities with my friends.

If you know anything about us women, parenting and motherhood is a touchy, fragile point on the spectrum of female hood in this century. Trying to keep a family, while being a working or stay-at-home parent, and feeling judged from all quarters is an emotionally fragile place to be. In friendships then, it becomes almost a taboo subject. For a woman like me who believed in the spirit of authenticity, in how it takes a village to raise a child, and who would want my friends to step in and correct my future child if they were ever on the wrong path, I found my worldviews at odds with that of some of my close friends. They had no fault in this. I had presumed we had plenty in common, based on the seven friendship pillars. That is, until children arrived on the scene.

It appeared like someone had handed me a crystal ball and I was peering into it and seeing the friends we were slowly blurring into the distance. Funny thing was every time I would mention in some friend groups, about my feelings on the changing quality of our relationships, I would be met with counterpoints. Statements to the effect that perhaps I was expecting too much out of the friend group, that people were busy, to reach out more myself, or better yet to take everything in my stride. Yet, I could not shake the nagging feeling that we, and things were no longer the same. Or was it I who had changed and did not know it?

THE BELONGING PARADOX

A Pandemic and A Ghostly Vision of Friendship

Stories about the COVID-19 pandemic and its effects on our lives have become almost cliché. You may have heard and read endless accounts of how for many introverts, it was a much-needed break from a world that would not stop talking. As someone who leans very much on the introverted side, who recharges and gets respite from being alone, the forced time alone during the pandemic was paradoxically traumatic. As good things go, it was also during that forced season of introspection born of the type of internalized loneliness that I would never wish on anyone, that the whispers of this book began floating into my subconscious. Whispers that got so loud, I could no longer ignore them.

A writer I admire greatly once wrote a piece titled, "*It's Your Friends Who Break Your Heart*", probably in a riff of the popular idea of romantic partners causing us heartbreaks. Her essay homed in on the noticeable fact that the older we get, the more we need friends, but the harder it is to make and to keep them.[e] I could not agree more, because, during the pandemic, not only did we experience the world shutting down, but I along with so many others, experienced a shutting down of my friend world.

I can look back now and think perhaps it was us shrinking in fear at the uncertainty, not knowing if the world was going

---

[e] Jennifer Senior, "It's Your Friends Who Break Your Heart." *The Atlantic*, February 9, 2022. www.theatlantic.com/magazine/archive/2022/03/why-we-lose-friends-aging-happiness/621305/

to end with all of us pillaged by this unknown virus. I am a woman though, for whom if and when the world is going to end, I would want to face it in a blaze of glory with my friends, spouse included as chief friend. In reality, the pandemic and subsequent stay-at-home orders blurred this glorious vision to a point where I could not understand what was happening and what if any lessons were to be learned. Because the degree of ghosting from people I called friends is still an explanation-defying mystery. A mystery I hope would not require a second lockdown period to solve.

> *Growing up, I did not know I was an introvert. We had no such tools as are available now for personality typing. I just know I have always been an observer in social groups and settings. I have come to discover that this tends to make people uncomfortable because they cannot easily categorize you. But on the other hand, I believe neither can they easily manipulate. Because of this I have always been an outsider, never really belonging. It is uncomfortable at times, to be outside of the circle or a group because insecure people seem to want to be in control of others, and they will manipulate to get their way even if it means using deception and I always seemed to be a target of exclusionary behaviors from such people probably because they could not type me. How did it make me feel? I think when people go out of their way to exclude me it is still uncomfortable, but I am good with not being included in some places. I also appear not to be a "natural fit" in other spaces, so it does not bother me to be excluded. I have learned to like myself and my own company.*
>
> ~ *SA*

THE BELONGING PARADOX

A Connector Disconnected

A few years ago, if anyone had asked what my relationships archetype was, I would have emphatically proclaimed that I was a connector. I still think I am one, and I consider it a gift to be used in the service of others. However, I am certainly not as affirmingly proclamatory about it as I once was.

This 'connector' archetype comes from my love for synthesis, of connecting and joining, be it ideas, or people. Although I am an introvert who gets her energy from being alone, I also love people hugely, in one-on-one doses. I have come to know a lot of people through the years through many different avenues. And because of my joy of connecting, I have been able to bring many people and friends of friends together. Once I make a mental match of possible pillars of connection, I make an introduction and leave it to all parties to see what they can make out of the connection.

So, while it looked like I knew so many people and had very healthy six degrees of connection all around, I only had a few people I considered to be in my inner friend circle. In this though, there was one question I never really stopped to ponder, probably even ignoring certain evidence in front of me because I had learned (through cognitive behavioral practices), to reframe unhelpful thoughts. That question was one of reciprocity.

> ## The Reciprocity Question
>
> "If I considered a person a part of my Dunbar's number of 5 (close friend) and they in turn considered me in the number of 15 (good friend), then where exactly was our friendship within those concentric circles?"

This principle of reciprocity in relationships is a topic that I have seen adult women tend to discount. I believe it lets us off the hook too easily in terms of what we are owed, or what we owe our friends in terms of time and other voluntary commitments to a relationship that we both chose (hopefully). For some, the change of heart about the relationship and perhaps any necessary endings are harder than they would like. Therefore, they think, the next best thing is to cut off contact for (ghost) relationships that they do not want to continue investing in, without thought that the discomfort may in fact be double-sided. This mismatch in placement hierarchy and subsequent relationship demise was probably what I experienced during the pandemic, as did so many others. Either way, it was something I needed to come to terms with as related to state belonging in my relationships. And you can call me soppy for saying this; But I love my girlfriends and I love friendships. Friendship is an overarching core value for me. I want to be able to have an enduring girl-posse of friends.

Even as I declared my wants and desires for high quality friendships, I had to face my reality. In coming to terms during this period of grieving the abrupt loss of many friendly relationships, I wondered:

1) Was I not a good friend?
2) Did I overestimate my contributions to reciprocity in relationships?
3) Was I too lofty in my aspirations as to what a friend should be (and did I need to lower the bar in terms of expectations about friendships)?

While I still do not have all the answers, I did use a cognitive behavioral framework to process the evidence before me and to think through these questions.

♦♦♦♦♦

To the first question, I knew that I was a good friend. I had been told so on multiple occasions by multiple people over the course of my life. For the second, I most likely overestimated my contributions. As humans, we like to think we are good people, and I am no exception. I was aware though that my own busy life taking care of children and going through some tough seasons at work had caused a shift in how I showed up in friendship conversations.

I did not want to be that friend who would go on interminably about the vicissitudes of life and work and then turn around and not do anything about it. Which is to say, I knew the effects of listening to negative conversations from people all around me, and I was trying to limit myself from whining while I worked through things. The painful realization that I was becoming that complaining friend made me pull back until I could get a lid on it. In trying to rein in the external sequela of inner wounds, I found myself in a sort of wilderness season. The thing, though, about wilderness experiences is that while you are gone, the folks you left behind make new friends. Also, you are never going to be the same person you were before the wilderness season.

The season away (and apart) from people led to a resolution of the third question, having had time in the extended stillness to reframe what friendship looked and felt like. I realized that I did in fact need to reset my expectations. Such that in returning to the friendship arena, I was able to enter with a renewed sense of self, forged through seasons of aloneness.

THE BELONGING PARADOX

Of Gap Years and Making Friends. Going All Out

While I write primarily from the perspective of an introverted, neurodivergence-aware adult woman, the shrinking friendship circles over time can also happen to extroverted persons if they do not actively maintain their connections. Although, I find that some extroverts are really just social extroverts and instead lean more toward introversion in their inner lives. In which case we can call these kinds of people, ambiverts. In this vein, I have seen the friendship circle shrink happen with an extrovert like my spouse (my polar opposite in terms of introversion). After marriage, over time, his friends it appeared, began to disappear. But being the quintessential extrovert, he still manages to foster ephemeral friendships, something I am learning to do, from observing him.

For the introverts among us then, filling in the gaps for relationship and friendship health, would require going out into the community and serving and meeting other people in many third spaces through intersecting interests and commonalities. I have been for example, to make friends at my children's schools, and at their various extracurricular activities.

·····

Presently I have a band of Caribbean and African American moms as a big part of my friendship circle. We all met while our kids were in a private faith-based K-12 academy. One of them, who we call our social connecting thread had asked for all our numbers at an end-of-school event and planned a potluck for us. At this potluck, we all discovered that we each had our individual experiences of othering from the new white lady principal at our children's school that year.[f] The school had recently undergone a change of leadership and the wonderful Black woman we met as principal, who had welcomed us all so warmly had been asked to step down, and we all felt the gap she left behind.

As part of getting to know each other better, some of us in the group committed to reading clubs, and regular Saturday morning walks where we talk through life and work issues. All of this required intentionality from us as we continue working our way through the different friendship levels (and pillars), per Dunbar's study. Even with our very busy lives as working moms, when the time came to show up, dress up, or shout out for us or for our children, we did it fiercely, and we still do, and this with so much respect for one other. Which to me, is all a part of living the good life as a woman in these parts. (This same band of moms, in the summer of 2021, when we were still social distancing, came to support Child 1 with a drive-through for his first lemonade stand. They cheered and clapped at his enterprising spirit and at the end, he made a cool $400, according to him. If that is not social support and belonging in action, then I do not know what is).

---

[f] Othering: *the act of treating someone as though they are not part of a group and are different in some way,* in Cambridge English Dictionary, https://dictionary.cambridge.org.

THE BELONGING PARADOX

> *So many of us enrolled our children in the school precisely because of the welcoming nature of the former principal who was a delightful Black woman. We were crushed to realize that the experience of being ignored or looked over by the new principal who happened to be a white woman, was not unique to each of us. By the end of that school year, all but one of us had unenrolled our children partly due to the accumulation of these incidents. We later learned the principal had been moved but by then, our children had been well situated in other schools. I remember thinking, in what world do you pay school fees for a child in private school and still get treated so poorly. We all decided at different times, in different ways to speak. We spoke with our monies and took our kids to other schools.*
>
> *I learned that sometimes you do not need to speak or interact physically to make your absence felt in certain spaces. You can and should let your money speak.*
>
> ~ *SD*

⬥⬥⬥⬥⬥

Other friendships we use to fill belonging gaps are work friends, although this comes easier for some than others. Making work friends is also dependent on the types of colleagues one is fortunate to work with, and in what areas or industries one finds themselves. Continually existing with people who practice unhealthy competition and transactional behaviors at work can be a shock to the nervous system.

Learning to recognize such environments quickly and create your own social networks of uplift and support is critical to stabilizing one's sense of belonging.

In my opinion, part of life coaching in societies where the culture is more individualistic, and capitalist should be to encourage people to reflect on their values (see the Belonging Practices chapter). To not make a point of settling into certain industries where people with Machiavellian and other dark triad personalities abound. Or industries with an abundance of a scarcity mentality. This coaching is crucial for those who consider themselves people-persons and for those raised in more collectivist societies, because it enables effective bridging of cultural differences. One thing I know for sure is that, when we enter the workforce from a place of stable belonging, we are able to create effective boundaries, choosing how to make and keep work friends in a healthy way. The next section will speak more to belonging at work.

THE BELONGING PARADOX

Looking for Friends. Good Friends

We can build back belonging in friendships.[d] What the pandemic helped me understand on a visceral level, was the difference between various measures of closeness. I used to associate closeness with a feeling, but friendship researchers speak of behavioral interactions; how people should behave in a close relationship.[6] There should be a discrete amount of time spent together—whether virtual or in person—shared activities, and mutual influence. (This may be why we think people at work should be our friends because we sometimes share these three things in common).

A close friendship should consist of both feelings and behaviors. I always say, feelings alone cannot fuel us. If you have a person who makes you feel good when you are with them, who only checks on you once a year, but checks in on others monthly, such a one you realize very quickly, is not the friend they say they are, despite how they make you feel. Because their behavior is lagging behind any purported shared feelings.

The work we must do then as we get older, when the propensity to lose friendships is so much higher, is to ensure quality friendships over quantity. Doing the work to ensure that the friendships we want to keep within our inner circles are high quality ones is not easy. We owe it to our friends and to ourselves to make sure that none of the dimensions of

---

[d] Alex Williams, We Want Our Friends Back! (But Which Ones?). *The New York Times.* March 27, 2021. www.nytimes.com/2021/03/27/style/coronavirus-friends-winnowing.html

closeness falls out of alignment. Doing this will require consciously bringing our friendships into valuation. When I speak of valuation, it may sound like something day traders do. With friendship valuation, it means to honestly count what a friendship means to us. We must place value on something to invest in it. I have a saying that I made popular in my friend group, "People make time for what is important to them." A statement I have seen play out, time and again in relationships.

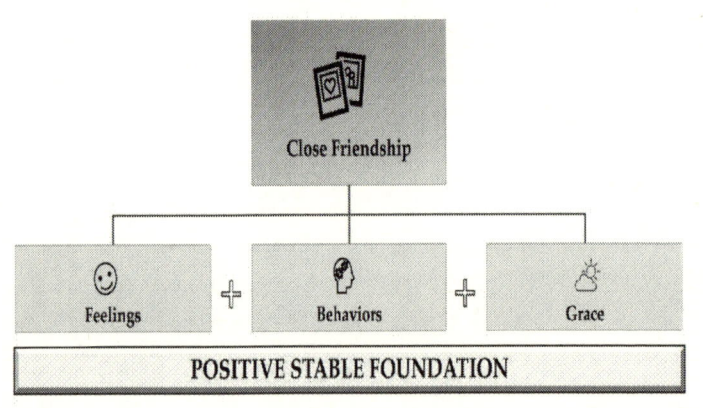

Three pillars marking the positive foundation for close friendships

Friendship and Belonging: How to Valuate and Invest

In terms of valuation and reciprocity, if you value a friendship and you do not mind that said friend does not spend as much time with you as you do with them, then all is well. Do not end the relationship simply because you think time spent must be equally balanced. Only you can determine the worth of your valuations for each of your friendships.

THE BELONGING PARADOX

After valuation, comes the investment. In this case, of your resources in the form of effort; thought, time, and gift giving. The gift giving here does not have to cost a ton of money but will cost some effort. Remember, if we were to speak about things of value, in acquisition terms, it costs less to keep the things we already have (in terms of maintenance) than it does to go out and acquire new ones. Same with our friendships. Making the time and effort to keep and maintain our long-term friendships can yield a greater return on investment in terms of intimacy, tolerance, and forgiveness of our faults and failings, when compared with someone who is just getting to know us.

Grace Giving in Friendship

I cannot speak about belonging and friendship without speaking about grace (see The BELONG framework at the end of this book). Giving grace; to ourselves and to those in our friend circles in terms of personality quirks. I for one have always sensed that I was somewhat neurodivergent. Even as a young girl I tended toward 'a lot'—a lot of talking, a lot of wanting to hang out with friends, and the attendant outsized feelings of rejection whenever I sensed unevenness in group dynamics. This interesting combination can only fit in with those it can fit in with. As a result, every time a friendship ended, or did not go the way I wanted, I would mourn and ruminate on it for weeks and months on end (I still do but not as much). It was not until I sat and answered the three questions I posed earlier. Only then, did I find a measure of relief.

•••••

Since ghosting can appear like presumptive rejection, I know I may never be able to explain certain things regarding my experience of it. Instead, I give myself grace to keep working on finding and keeping friends with whom I can be myself. I give myself grace too as I work on being that friend for others. I hope you get to give yourself the same gift of grace because it is going to be so worth the price.

Belonging Corner Reflections

1) What do you think about belonging in friendships? Do you think it is something we need to be aware of? If so, how would you measure your degree of belonging in different friendships?
2) How do you think your personality has influenced your belonging in your friendships to date? Did it influence your ability to begin and end friendships in various life stages?
3) Are you aware of how you influence belonging for those in your friendship circles? Do you work toward ensuring mutual reciprocity in your friendships?
4) How would you bring belonging into the friendships and relationships you currently desire to build or maintain?

PART III

Belonging at Work

People have a long history of trading money for belonging

— Seth Godin

Work takes up so much of our life. Even if we do not outrightly state it, many of us want work that is meaningful and purposeful and generative in terms of the environment we work in. For young and older adults alike, a sense of belonging at work is part of how we consider ourselves initiated into a work environment.

If you are, or know a young adult navigating the world of work, or of graduate school, or even of both, like I once had to, what is it like for you? Did you attempt to join your new gang, your gang of co-workers that is? If you did, how did it work out for you? If you are right now in the middle of work life and you are observing certain incongruences and contemplating follow-up questions to your observations, I would say, keep observing, but keep living and participating because there is no way out but through. The robustness of the social resources acquired in this life stage has the capacity to see you and I through many coming days and nights.

If you are long past the young adult stage, no fear, there is a lot about turning unsavory experiences around and making them work well. Belonging is something we can give ourselves at work.

Young Adults Divide. Then Unite

Relationships that lead to a healthy sense of belonging are crucial at all life stages, but no more so than in emerging adulthood.[1] The stage when responsibilities become a part of everyday life and one can no longer afford to hand over the wheel to parents to take care of things. Entering into a new social sphere, whether of education as in graduate school for those who choose that path, or of a new job in higher income brackets, can be angst inducing. So many questions gnaw at us. Questions like: Will I succeed? Will I be good enough to make it? Will I be able to make friends?

Feeling like we are not good enough for where we find ourselves has been a topic of research and writing for the past few decades. This, based on research on Impostor Phenomenon (IP) in white suburban professional women by Dr Pauline Clance who found that the highly accomplished women in her study were a worried lot. Worrying that people would think they did not merit their social status and that they attained their professional successes by fraudulence. According to Dr Clance, she heard these kinds of statements, over and again. She gave this observation a name, she called it Impostor Phenomenon.[2] I bring up this concept because feelings such as those reported by Dr Clance in her Impostor Phenomenon Scale, can interfere with a young working adult's sense of belonging in professional settings.

There will not be enough room to tell stories of people and places of belonging. These wonderful stories can be such an intrinsic part of our lives, that we do not take much note of them. It is the stories of non-belonging that fuel something in

THE BELONGING PARADOX

us. These are the ones that make us vow to ensure that others do not go through the same things we went through.

Stories in this section, reflect on and how I and others have understood and lived through non-belonging (and belonging) at work. This is intentional, for good measure. Especially for those who might be living through their own story presently and wondering if there is anything wrong with them and why they seem to be having these experiences. I want to shout out loud from the rooftops that there is nothing wrong with you. There is nothing that an increased understanding of societal norms, cultures, and ways of being cannot explain and bring some comfort.

As a prime example, after graduating pharmacy school, I worked for an international consulting firm. In order to be considered for employment, we had to take a job aptitude test (JAT). You were called back for a series of interviews, only if you passed the aptitude test. These tests, with their binary nature (pass or fail) were objective in that they did not require candidates second-guessing themselves about being called for interviews and the like. These days though, when I consider recruiting systems, I wonder if aptitude tests ought to make a comeback. The failures of job hunting with modern-day recruiting systems cannot be placed in the laps of the individual job seeker. This example bears mentioning because a lack of success in job searches can potentially contribute to feelings of non-belonging in emerging and young adults trying to find their way in the world of work.

The Glory of the Latter Days

The first two jobs I had after pharmacy school (at a hospital first and the consulting firm above) are a standard that I have used to measure belonging in other workspaces. For the hospital, I had been deployed there for a year of mandatory service work, the staff were few and we needed to work together, so we did it. Being one of two women among all men was an experience in feeling cared for at work. Perhaps, it also being a temporary work situation helped as the year came and went too quickly. The consulting firm on the other hand was a delight of a workplace. That it was an American company in the heart of Lagos, Nigeria made for many dreams about how wonderful it would be to work in America itself, a dream that is still materializing.

Psychologists talk about the concept of our present self and our experiencing self and how our experiencing self is prone to skewed narratives. Which is to say that we tend to fondly remember many things that may not have been that glorious in the first place. This is also known as misremembering or memory infidelity, a phenomenon seen with the prevalence of false eyewitness accounts.[3] In fact, some researchers believe that our brains capacity for memory infidelity is a sign of optimal memory. I think about this whenever I recount my days in this consulting firm that was my initial foray into the corporate world as a young adult.

The evidence, however, from that period bears me witness that this firm was truly one of the best places to work at the time. I still have bosom friends (male and female) that I made in the two and a half years that I worked there. At the time, we had a completely open office workspace. Anyone could come in, plop their belongings on any seat, plug in their laptops and just get to work. You could almost never tell who the senior or junior employees were. Talk about the practice of an egalitarian work system right in the midst of the hierarchical work and school environment I had been raised in. In this organization, I saw so much brilliance, camaraderie, and good work ethics on display. Because no system is perfect, there were ups and downs, minor dramas and major personalities here and there. But in all, it was a respectful environment and employees thrived in that atmosphere. Speaking of open offices, I do not know if I can work in one presently. Things change, as the next chapters will show.

An Intro to Class Acts in Graduate School

After my stint in the corporate world, I relocated to the US for graduate school, where things began to unravel, thread by specious thread. My lived experience of culture shock will go without saying. Culture shock is a common enough experience for many immigrants, especially those who emigrated from low to lower-middle income economies to high income countries like the United States.[4]

The graduate school arm of the US academic-industrial complex was at the time (and still is) occupied predominantly by South and East Asians. The graduate program I was accepted into was no exception. Of the six or so students in my cohort, five were of Indian origins. And every year had their numbers increasing until there were about 11 of them (of 14 students). I did not foresee a problem with this initially because I reasoned we were all there to study and to do as best we could within the dictates of the program. Besides, program diversity was not my business.

But, by the second year of the program, it became more and more apparent that it was impossible to break into the tightly knit cluster that these Indian students had formed by way of ethnic affiliations. They had a study group as I belatedly discovered. I asked to be included in the group and never got a response from any one even after repeatedly asking. The other strange observation to me at that time was that certain colleagues from their country were also excluded from these study groups, and other joint activities. I could not understand it, for the life of me. It was not until we had another student from my own country get admitted into the program. She had made fast friends with another Indian girl who it also appeared had been shut out of the in-group. It was from both of these women that I finally came to some semblance of understanding.

This fellow country woman of mine (now longtime girlfriend) made a remark, the day I finally decided to ask if she was also having the experience of not being invited to activities. She exclaimed, "Otito, do you not realize that Indians have a very strong caste system, and what you are noticing and experiencing is a vestige of that system that they brought here with them." "I know because my Indian friend told me more about the system and identified those from the upper-class and those from the untouchable classes among all our student colleagues." She continued, "Do you not see how one of them is almost revered and can get away with anything? "It's because she's a Brahmin, a member of the upper-class caste. Such and such are Dalits. This other person, and their spouse appear to be the untouchables, hence the marked disparities in their interactions with one another."[5] Talk about a Duh! moment.

◆◆◆◆◆

Did I know anything about the caste system? Of course I did. I am an Igbo girl. The same tribe as those famous Nigerian writers, China Achebe and Chimamanda Ngozi Adichie to name but two. I do not mean to place myself in the company of these outstanding writers, I use them only as examples of tribal affiliation.

As an Igbo girl, I grew up knowing that I was an *Nwadiala* or a true-born daughter of the soil. Which meant that there were people who were not originally conceived to be real born (either daughters or sons). These were people, whether through sins of omission and commission or by accidents of birth (if born into such families) did not belong. These people were called *Osu,* in what is now very thankfully a defunct caste system. This defunctness is not a mere historical fact, because it still existed as recently as 2021, in some parts of Igbo land. This caste system, as others like it was one of social hierarchy and segregation, with the forbidding of inter-caste marriages and all other forms of ostracism that came with it.

While I knew about the Osu system through books, and through oral history from my parents, I never actually knew a person who was shunned or ostracized based on the system. Everyone attended school, and played and ate together. To us, it was simply a system that existed in the past and many modern-day Igbo like me wanted nothing to do with it.

"So, yes Ma'am, I was aware of caste systems, thank you."

My dismay came from the thought (or reality?) that people could actually bring traditions and social systems from their country of birth into a new one, and consciously or unconsciously impose them on people from other parts of the world. Adding insult to injury was the fact that we were all immigrants trying to make our way in this new country with its own system of unspoken rules and cultural ways of being.

The realization about my student colleagues' cultural practices, however late, helped me a lot. I hope the mental models developed from this helps you too as you navigate your way in the world.

THE BELONGING PARADOX

> *"Sometimes, peoples' perceived social rejection of us has nothing to do with us. Their cultural practices or ways of being, which is all they have ever known, can get in the way of making room for others and helping others feel included."*

These Indian colleagues were simply being Indian in their behaviors born out of their social systems. The rest of us just happened to be in the way.

It should be clear that I am not making excuses for them. Especially since they were going to graduate and become leaders and future change makers in the outside world. The need for students like these to increase their cultural intelligence is even higher than I would ascribe to the average American person. I also do not excuse them, knowing that they were, like me, hoping to work and live in a country supposedly built on the constitutional idea that ALL men [women?] were born equal, with inalienable rights.

My coworker and I were in a meeting with our boss who is of Indian descent. My coworker is also of Indian descent, and we all worked in an organization that was made up mainly of people from Southeast Asia. That had concerned me a little because it lacked diversity, but I just kept an open mind.

During this meeting, I reported on my completed tasks to our boss and further explained how I was excited to do more and provide even more updates. Our boss ignored me and directed follow-up questions to my coworker and even assigned her new tasks based on my just reported updates. My coworker was confused but kept her calm. I also said nothing. After the meeting, I checked in with my colleague and shared how I felt ignored during the meeting. She confirmed that it felt like our boss had indeed ignored me despite the fact that I did the work and provided the update. It just felt like she didn't want to reckon with me. It was weird. I had to have a conversation with the people in HR, who mediated a resolution.

Whether or not the boss had something against me, the fact that most people in the organizational unit were of a certain ethnicity, and I am now more aware about their cultural dispositions makes me understand better now why nothing about working in the space felt welcoming. My boss's actions made me feel like she deliberately chose to ignore my presence and refuse to reckon with me.

In reflecting about this so many years later, I think, "Did she ignore and undermine me? Yes." "Was it intentional?" I will never know!"

~ KA

THE BELONGING PARADOX

Lab Work Compatibility

In the lab where I worked on my doctoral thesis, it was quite a different story. My primary graduate advisor was an Indian woman. My other advisor, a white man, it turned out had married an Indian woman. These two individuals helped buoy me through the initial disorientation of attending graduate school after so many years past undergrad. When I decided to change my initial field of study and combine majors, they supported my advocacy for a new field to accommodate me who did not find a fit in any programs being offered then.

That primary advisor? She was only a year older than me, but I observed her run that lab as professionally as one could ask for in terms of parity and fairness. There we were, two young women, trying to make our way in a country with different ideals and different cultures from the ones we were born into. We both dug in and worked our behinds off for various reasons. For I, who was there to get my degree, I needed to show I was capable of earning my way in the eyes of this brilliant Indian woman who could have been my sister. But with whom I could not shake off the darned feeling that she did not think too highly of people from my part of the world, due to that deeply entrenched caste system. I am not saying she treated me any way other than professionally. I just could not make out what it was between her and I in terms of a mentoring relationship. She, on the other hand needed to advance her fledgling career, get grants and other hallmarks needed to be a successful academic professional.

So, we needed each other, she and I. This superordinate goal for both of us, I believe made for a successful graduate student-advisor relationship. I was thrilled when she made tenure. My working in her lab made me realize we can set aside differences and just get sh*t done. But the expectations were clear from the beginning for us, that was this was going to be a work relationship. That we would get all our work done and then have our annual end of year or Christmas lab party when due. A 'work first, play later' philosophy.

Without her knowing it, she taught me how to be a real boss because I never saw or perceived any in-group favoritism from her. If anything, as can be common with many immigrants, she preferred not to work with students from her part of the world where possible, in order to avoid the perception of nepotism. This meant she was sometimes sterner with the Indian students in the lab, holding them to really high standards.

Speaking of cultural knowledge, I cannot speak only about unsavory social customs, I must also speak about the beauty of them. Food, and eating together at a table is a known cross-cultural glue. From these students in this regard, I learned about different types of rice from regions in India. I also ate the best chicken Biryani I have ever eaten in my life (and I make a good Biryani these days) from the kitchen of my secondary advisor's mother-in-law. I love good food, cooking and eating it and I was glad to have been exposed to this side of the Indian culture too.

THE BELONGING PARADOX

Post-Graduation: A Cross-Country Move

I got married during graduate school, a thing my primary advisor insinuated was going to be a distraction from my work. At which I wondered (as I am prone to do), whose career was at stake. Hers or mine? Not only did I get married, but I also had a baby right before my dissertation defense and graduation, a decision I have never regretted, for obvious reasons. Life waits for no one, not least me.

After the birth of my child, I became a stay-at-home mother for a total of 14 months. I did this by choice, knowing that I would never get the time back to be just a mother once I entered the workforce. We managed our precarious financial state as single-income (growing) family until a year and half later when I accepted a postgraduate fellowship in Nashville Tennessee.

While I was thrilled to have been accepted into this prestigious fellowship, working as a postdoctoral associate was not what I had envisioned; it was a bit boring, if I am being honest. We were left to our dealings, which one could sum up in two major activities; research and write papers. What else would I have come there to do might be a question? My brain as it was wired, simply needed more variety and stimulation for sure.

♦♦♦♦♦

Despite this workplace ennui, I considered myself to be winning in the friendship arena, having made wonderful new friends, one of them a male Nigerian colleague who was also in the fellowship program. The researcher life did get upended a bit when my primary advisor left to go back to the Midwest where he was from. If you are thinking, "Another primary advisor?" Know that scientific training is replete with these advisor-advisee or so-called mentor-mentee relationships, where one often had no idea what you were being mentored on.

This primary advisor was a white man, who took a chance on me, having never met me. This man, who once told me that I was too sassy. I remember asking him which of the two definitions of sassy he meant as I preferred to go with 'bold and audacious' as opposed to 'impudent and insolent'. To which he shook his head at me, saying that my response was exactly what he was referring to.

We fell out, him and me, because this man lied to my face by denying something in public that he had told me behind closed doors. I saved that face by claiming that I had misremembered the incident. But it marked the beginning of our subsequent split. A split that turned into a chasm when he, without being asked, told my program director that he did not think I was ready to do a master's degree, an associated benefit available to those who chose to do it, based on the terms of the fellowship. He insinuated that I just wanted the master's degree for the sake of it and that I had not shown true commitment.

I, who had gone to look for partial funding on my own so my program would not have to bear the full costs of my crossing over to another department for this master's degree. This same advisor who had told me that his primary goal of

THE BELONGING PARADOX

doing a PhD while in medical school was so he could take advantage of the loan forgiveness program on offer and not leave medical school with debt. To then sit and pontificate about what I was deserving or not deserving of based on his own subjective bases, I did not take kindly to at all.

While I wished him well when he was leaving, I am sure he had an inkling that this sassy female advisee was not a fan of the paternalism he had tried to display. In retrospect, I suppose I could have been more circumspect in my conversations seeing as I was a Black girl with a white male boss. But the question would always remain, to what ends would that have taken me?

I would never know.

Working Two Jobs. For the Bills, and Non-belonging

While in Tennessee, I also worked as a pharmacist at a county medical center, an ethos of the need to have multiple options that I have followed to date. It was in the hospital environment here that I had my initial work non-belonging experience, a scar worse than the physical one from my cesarean section.

My second child was born at the same hospital where I worked. A place with a homogenous team of pharmacists who had been raised in the South. I was the first Black pharmacist they had employed in a long time, if ever, according to the pharmacy technician who was surprised to see me in a white coat on my first day of training. This place was such that, the HR specialist who onboarded me, when I introduced myself as being from the pharmacy department, presumed I was a pharmacy technician before I corrected the assumption (for which she apologized). All of this to say, the inter-group differential effect was evident in many ways and nowhere did I see it more than with my pregnancy experience and its aftermath.

As a woman from Nigeria, it was not customary for us to announce or talk about a pregnancy until the baby "settled". This practice was presumably to avoid the surrounding shame as well as save face for the woman in case of a miscarriage. But from an American perspective and culture, oversharing of pregnancy news, it appeared, was a thing. I had colleagues come with news of positive pregnancy tests and their initial six-week ultrasound scans. Perhaps then, the perceived lack of

THE BELONGING PARADOX

vulnerability from me not sharing my own news until after 20 weeks may have been one reason for the feeling of otherness I perceived from these female co-workers.

•••••

My baby was born in that hospital, via scheduled C-section on a Friday morning. A fact my colleagues knew, because I told them. Yet not a single one came to say hello to me, or the newborn. Of course, they could have just been thinking we needed our privacy and that visits to a colleague in a post-birth state was inappropriate. This is the nature of things with cultural worldviews.

After we returned home, I received a gift card in the mail, to the tune of $50, from this team of predominantly women pharmacists. I later learned that it was one individual who had got this card and sent it on behalf of the team. All this happened in a place where I had seen pictures of visits to other colleagues who had also given birth at this same hospital. I had witnessed them plan lavish showers for other colleagues, events to which I had always contributed my dollar quotient. It was a strange situation to observe, this thing that happened to me.

And this is what bothers me about uneven social dynamics. Anyone to whom the story above is told without context would probably have asked what I did to deserve that kind of treatment from colleagues. And this would have been the wrong question to ask of the person being othered. I say this because I who had experienced this, also had contrary evidence to this type of group behavior, based on my experience with giving birth to my first-born child when I worked at another hospital system in Pennsylvania. I knew therefore, that this could not have been just about me, and about what I did or did not do. Rather it was more about the spirit of the place and the team represented there.

In terms of inter-group dynamics, this Tennessee group of co-workers probably saw nothing wrong in not celebrating the arrival of my baby, because of the lack of close friendship bonds between them and me. Which is to say, this was not about liking or hating. I was just not a member of their in-group.

♦ ♦ ♦ ♦ ♦

Invitation to Baby shower 1 (created by Mr. L)

THE BELONGING PARADOX

A Country Criss-Cross of Work Belonging Memories

This was not the case with the women pharmacists at the hospital in Pennsylvania. Because us humans due to the significance we place on negative experiences are prone to remembering more of our non-belonging stories. I must now contrast my Tennessee experience with that of the wholesome belonging experiences with the birth of my first baby.

At this hospital where I interned, while still in graduate school, to accumulate my mandatory 1500 hours for pharmacist licensure requirements. My preceptor, a white woman, who had only recently taken up this role due to a sudden dramatic change in organizational leadership, along with two other pharmacists, came together and hosted the most lavish baby shower for me. They bought my baby so many gifts, that to this day, I am overcome with emotion whenever I think about their kindness and generosity. I think about how they did not have to do this, being that I was just a volunteer student intern.

I also had another baby shower planned by my graduate advisors and many faculty and students participated to make it a beautiful day. Then, I had a third surprise baby shower from my family and friends at home. I always say my first baby came into a world where there had been so much love showered on him, pre-birth, that he had no choice than to be the most effusive and friendly baby that he turned out to be.

I shared these experiences to say that I knew what belonging and communal love for an expectant mom looked and felt like because I had seen it in action, not once, but thrice. This was how I knew that what I experienced at work in Tennessee was out of place. The felt experience of belongingness from Philadelphia was what bolstered me when I decided to pay if forward and plan a beautiful shower for one of my postdoctoral research lab colleagues—this Chinese girl, who I realized was going to be left alone to her dealings—as she prepared to welcome a new baby. She later told me that no one had ever done anything like that for her before. On my end, I was only glad to play a part in a sweet entrance for a newborn coming into our world.

Cutting shower 2 baby cake in the graduate student conference room

THE BELONGING PARADOX

> *At work, I was the only Black person on my team, and there weren't many people who looked like me in the organization, so I never really felt like I belonged. However, my manager was always intentional about making sure I felt seen, valued, and treated like everyone else. One time, it was my birthday, and I had recently gotten my driver's license. She and my teammates gave me a very thoughtful gift related to being a new driver's license holder in the U.S. and a card with some of the kindest words I have ever received from colleagues.*
>
> *This gesture made me feel seen, valued, and equally important, especially because this was how the rest of the team was celebrated on their birthdays. I felt like I mattered.*
>
> *Because of this experience, I am very intentional about how I show up for others at work, especially if they come from different backgrounds.*
>
> *~KA*

The Tennessee experience is in the rear view now as I moved away to other workplaces. Still, speaking of celebrating people at work, I have observed the many ways in which people are subtly signaled as to whether they belong or not. Signals amplified by the magnitude of events planned around arrival of babies. Or around departures by way of resignations, or retirements, and even funerals. This is why I cannot but bring up the principle of procedural justice at work for practices and customs such as the ones I mention here.[a]

---

[a] Procedural Justice, https://law.yale.edu/justice-collaboratory/procedural-justice

If there is going to be a custom or practice around gift giving or commiseration for life events, norms around this can be established by the leader, and early too, especially for smaller teams. Of course, without any of this being mandatory, since such customs are not official work benefits. Also, I am mindful of the fact that not everyone in an office or organizational unit can have and will have (or even want) a baby. On the other hand, when we realize that babies are an addition to a family, norms can also be set up around celebrating not just expectant mothers, but fathers too. To leave commemorations of life-defining events to 'office or work friends' to plan and execute can lead to massive exclusionary behaviors even if unintentional.

If we subscribe to a spirit of comradeship or esprit de corps at work and the various mantras about work being a family, it becomes even more crucial to recognize all members of that work-family as having equal value.

♦♦♦♦♦

I could not help asking my intern preceptor why she went out of the way to plan such a lavish shower. She told me that she considered it a part of her responsibility as a preceptor to take care of not only of my professional learning, but also social, and emotional learning. Well, she did not use those terms exactly, because social and emotional learning was not a buzz phrase at the time. I understood that she was saying her felt responsibility to me far surpassed the corporate one that had been suddenly foisted on her.

She had chosen to precept me when no one else would take the role after my previous preceptor, our pharmacy director, had been abruptly and unceremoniously walked out of the building one morning. The new leader, a Vietnamese woman, refused to supervise the completion of the few hundred hours left for my internship. According to her, she did not know me or know anything about the arrangement I had with my former preceptor.

At the time, I was too focused on not having my accumulated intern hours go to waste than place any focus on this supposed rejection. I asked her if I could find another pharmacist within our department to precept me. She said I could continue working there if I found someone. And that was how Essa, after hearing about my predicament, raised a hand on my behalf, and became a treasured mentor to this day. In looking back now, I realize I could not have faulted the new leader for her assessment of the situation and therefore of me. She truly did not know me on a personal level, even though she had been the Assistant Director of the pharmacy the time I was there. She probably did not wish to sink her reputation by taking on the intern of a "disgraced" predecessor.

I consider this now, as most other things, part of the circle of life. And if one was to think on it further, I did get what I wanted which was to complete my intern hours. When I factor in who eventually took on the preceptor role, I got even more than I bargained for, because my working with Essa turned out to be a huge blessing, and an ever-green example of how to offer belonging to others.

Belonging at Work

During the time that I worked at an establishment where I thought I had the opportunity to grow my career, I tried to participate in different events and activities within the organization but was met with 'brick walls'. It felt very much like I was a minority, and didn't belong in any of the outside non-work activities.

More than three quarters of the staff members were not familiar with working with a person of color, how much more someone with a non-English name.

I felt really frustrated and sometimes had what I now recognize as bouts of anxiety whenever I was scheduled to work.

I have learned that most people act the way they do based on what they have been exposed to. *So, if you find yourself in that type of environment, find your own social activities and people.*

~ SK

THE BELONGING PARADOX

A Warm Woman in Cold Work Climates

In 2015, I moved from Tennessee to New Jersey to begin work as an Assistant Professor in a new pharmacy school. Fresh out of postdoctoral studies, I must confess I did not quite know what I was doing. I was, however, determined to succeed in this new role because I had always desired the teaching side of my double-sided work as a researcher-educator. Within my first year, I also began working as a pharmacist at a multisite health care system.

My first three years at the primary job were idyllic. I had a boss (an Indian man, raised in East Africa) who it was obvious cared for everyone and advocated for us. To use words now being bantered around, I felt safe with this boss. There is nothing quite like knowing that the person who oversees your work wants the best for you.

All seemed to be going well until one sunny day in June 2018. We had gone out to a fancy restaurant to celebrate the end of the academic year. My boss got up to take a phone call, came back and told us he had to leave. And I never saw him again. At least not as a boss. It was over a year before he was able to meet for lunch. There, I witnessed this man's anguish as he recounted the story of an investigation being launched against him and how none of his bosses stood up for him. This incident with my boss and the lack of support he received at a crucial time was the first of many red flags, I encountered at work.

Prior to this, his former boss (the faculty dean) had been beaming out random signals of unapproachability in my direction. Whether through refusing to meet when I asked for meetings and asking me to go through the proper channels or asking him, my boss to talk to me about unverifiable reports she heard about me from other colleagues. I had ignored these red flags because I had a direct boss (a man) advocating for me. So, when this man had to resign unceremoniously, I felt like a house without a roof, rendered open to the elements. The new boss who took over, an East Asian male, was a man I was aware did not care for me and had shown me so categorically. I had once called out some inconsistencies in his work in leading a change management project when he tried pinning the reasons for this project on how some of my courses were taught. Either way, we all continued working as courteously and professionally as we could under the circumstances.

♦♦♦♦♦

The abrupt departure of my boss was an unexpected system change that took me a while to recover from. Now, you might wonder, "What's the big deal? It's just work. Anything can happen at work. Why are you so hung up on this?" And you would be right. The ball was on me to manage my expectations around work. But, you see, a part of me sensed that things would never be the same again at work because the strong advocate voice of my boss had been silenced.

Over the course of the next year, I debated a lot over leaving this job. By the end of the year, I talked myself out of it. I said things like, "Why would you leave a job because someone left?" "Are you using this as an excuse for escapism?" "You started something, you have to finish it." The last phrase from my inner voice won the day because prior to this, I had

THE BELONGING PARADOX

typically spent an average of three years at any job I had held due to boredom.

I was always moving, from one thing to another. From job to job to graduate school (which with its almost a 6-year tenure, felt endless) to postgraduate associate. With this new job then, I spent a lot of time overriding my nomadic instincts with some of the main things we tell ourselves. Things like, "You are an adult, now married with children." "Stop moving around so much." "Think about the family and don't be selfish." While these were all valid reasons, I sometimes look back and wonder what might have happened if I had followed the call of the wild heart that I was. Suffice to say, I stayed. From all that staying, came this book, with all the lessons learned.

Reflected Work Belonging States

I live in America. As a highly educated Black woman, entering certain rooms and spaces means you are sometimes the only one of your kind. While this observation has never really bothered me, I did prefer not to be the only (insert whatever traits here). Therefore, as I scoured listings for academic faculty roles, I would also look down the lists of faculty and staff photographs to make sure there was some representation of diversity. Despite knowing that having all white colleagues was not necessarily tied to one's belonging experience in a workplace, I did place value in seeing people from different parts of the world represented. So, when the offer from this private institution in a metropolitan part of the country came in the Spring of 2015, with what appeared to be a moderately diverse faculty and staff group, I took the job.

My first office door sign

THE BELONGING PARADOX

When COVID-19 hit us in 2020 and beyond was when I sensed, in terms of my state belonging, that I may have made a mistake staying at the job. I do not know what your work experience during the pandemic lockdown was and if you experienced anything like what I did at my job. During the almost 18 months of lockdown, not one person in the leadership team sent a message or note asking how we and our families were doing. Instead, they continued life as normal, making what appeared to be self-serving organizational changes. I thought to myself, what kind of a job am I at if the people I work with did not seem to care whether I lived or died. I understand that there was heightened anxiety all around. However, the first aspect of being a human-centered leader would have been to check in to see how your employees are faring. I must preface by saying, this was my experience. It could have been that others did not experience any of what I am writing here. Which then brings me to the concept of bosses having in-groups and out-groups. Even if I did not realize that I was in an out-group prior to this, the stay-at-home orders clarified this status for me.

I returned to work after the pandemic in the Fall of 2021 with a more conscious state of understanding regarding my co-workers. By this time, I had made tenure and obtained another graduate degree in organizational psychology. I chose this program because I wanted to learn more about human and organizational behaviors and leadership. I knew what I was experiencing on the job was not normal. I had experienced poor leadership and team behaviors across the multiple pharmacy departments I worked in over the years in various health systems in different regions of the country. I wondered if this was unique to the pharmacy profession, because if so, then it reflected poor leadership succession planning.

Over time, I realized that many pharmacy leaders become leaders based on their job competence and skills or based on sponsorship. As a result, many of them did not know how to lead people much less of leading diverse multicultural teams. They knew the technical aspects of the job and could do it well but the people skills were in many cases lagging. So, I went back to school to learn, teach, and apply. Completing that program was one of the highlights of being on the job for me. With this, I could continue to coach and teach as I had been doing. And with my newly acquired degree, it became even more obvious that what I had experienced and was experiencing was a heart- and people-centered leadership gap which subsequently translated into weak organizational cultures.

Culture fit is real. You can be in an organization or team and feel like an ugly duckling. For someone coming from a country that was socially oriented, where work was where you sometimes made bosom friends, where working together was often centered on both relationships and tasks. To come into workspaces where processes and products appeared to be prioritized over people was a major adjustment. I will take full responsibility for my mismatched expectations, as part of my present-day cultural awareness.

THE BELONGING PARADOX

On Being Considered a Diversity Number

One does not speak enough of certain pressures that can arise when issues of diversity enter workplace conversations. As a Black person, you do not want to presume that every other Black or other ethnically diverse professional wants to affiliate with you (see story about my Indian colleagues in grad school), so you initially may keep your distance, and they in turn keep theirs. Until you find other points of bonding interests.

I have had work experiences where I did make friends with people from my birth country (or other Black women) but got into trouble based on the perception that one was not being professional at work. At one of the hospitals where I once worked, a Chinese colleague had reported to our supervisors that I and another Nigerian colleague had spent the whole day chatting in vernacular and did not work on any of our extra-role responsibilities (this was a completely fabricated story). The manager rather than asking for our side of the story, emailed us about the need to ensure that this did not happen again. I responded in the affirmative and let her know I had taken note. When my Nigerian colleague asked me why I did not respond to correct the facts, I told her I thought it was a waste of energy (and time) to correct facts with a manager who would believe such a report and not bother to find out our side of the story. And besides, I replied, "The manager had access to the system work reports to see if we were truly not working "all day" during our eight-hour shift."

I do not believe that conversations about organizational citizenship behaviors (extra work responsibilities), should be had in the same way as those for policy and procedure deviations.[b] The manager could have had this conversation in-person to hear our story and let us know what her expectations were for the future. This way it did not come across as othering, in the sense that we (the two Black women), our language and our supposed indolence, were the problem. Never mind that our Chinese colleague could have had a [courageous] conversation with us and did not need to escalate an issue that we were in the dark about.

---

[b] Organizational Citizenship Behavior: Benefits and Best Practices; www.aihr.com/blog/organizational-citizenship-behavior/

THE BELONGING PARADOX

Your Contributions Are Valued. True for Some But Not All

I cannot write about my (and others) work experiences without writing about organizational culture and leadership. Our experience of work can be made or marred based on who we work with and who we work for. I had grown up around mentors who were working in a university system, and admired the autonomy they had in what they could and could not do as it related to their research endeavors.

So, when I chose the academic life, a life of the mind as I knew it, despite the abysmal pay, it was based on the premise of flexibility and autonomy. I know when we speak of autonomy as college teachers, people think we do nothing all day aside from teach one or two classes and the rest is free time. No one counts the amount of preparation for every single class, and for those who have to grade written papers, the amount of time this can take outside of regular hours. This autonomy too often can translate to a lack of work-life boundaries if one is not careful, because students (and colleagues) presume they can email you at odd hours. When you enforce off-the-clock boundaries, it can then lead to vitriolic student evaluations, either due to mismatched expectations, to entitlement or perhaps a combination of both.

I conceived of the ivory tower as a place where a meeting of minds would occur for me and those I worked with. Even as we worked to train the next set of professionals, that we would work together toward a common goal of getting our students educated and ready to face their professional world. What I met instead was what I now consider a community of minds quite alright, just not the kind I had in mind. In this particular 'tower', trying to offer different perspectives and clarifying opinions at faculty meetings became a Herculean task, without any aid. Many of my colleagues did not bother to speak up about issues, perhaps reckoning it would make no difference. I could not understand why. Why were we academic faculty and yet could not speak up and speak out? Was it a fear of retribution or what?

It became obvious, although I should have realized sooner, that diverse voices and opinions, especially from a person like me, were not welcomed. And that was made clear to me in subsequent years.

THE BELONGING PARADOX

An Understanding of Workplace Belonging

It was around this time of experiencing such ostracism at work after my previous boss's departure and trying to make sense of it that I made an appointment to see a therapist. In the course of meeting with her over a year, she confirmed what I had always known in the recesses of my mind about my neurodivergence. Instead of being overwhelmed, it was like someone had finally shed light on an area of my life that to that date, I could not make sense of. And now it all began to make sense; my ability to notice the things that most did not, my oversized sense of justice and perceived fairness, my speaking up fearlessly about things I felt needed to be said, the extreme sensitivity to perceived rejection cues, my forgetfulness, my hyper-focus on the things I found interesting, my boredom at unstimulating work, my ability to juggle innumerable activities, and my taking on too much at once at multiple times in my life, the crash and burns after a period of extended creative efforts. My one year with her helped me better understand myself.

This understanding did not make life at work less of a burden. In fact, if anything, it would only become worse. Because for people with ADHD or high-functioning autism who have been able to make it to adulthood because of the structures around them as children and adolescents (my boarding school provided this), stress points abound. This stress, due to the various aspects of our intersectionality clashing differently in different spaces.

Where other colleagues of different ethnicities may be forgiven for their forgetfulness and irascibility, as a Black woman, a foreign graduate and immigrant, people like me tend to be met with multiple abrasions. Working with people who do not have the same interests and world views as you, people who do not understand you and make no efforts to do so, people who would rather fill gaps for what they do not know about you with suspicion and gossip. We go to work and pretend to be a different person. If you have ever worn pants on chafed skin, you know how much it can hurt. That constant feeling of "I need to take this garment off so my skin can breathe." All of this can take its toll on belonging in the workplace.

THE BELONGING PARADOX

On Non-Representation and Inclusion

One of the weirdest things about being in environments where signals of non-belonging are being beamed at you overtly and covertly is the feeling of isolation. Of thinking that you are alone in your issues, of thinking that it must be about you and not about your colleagues and/or friends. I used to think this way until the lockdown gave me the gift of clarity around workplace issues that have to do with people who are different. Whether different in the more visible traits (ethnicity and language) or in the invisible ones that come with neurodivergence.

♦ ♦ ♦ ♦ ♦

During the lockdown two incidents happened. Over the course of one weekend, a man was murdered by the police because of a counterfeit twenty-dollar bill.[c] I also bore witness to a public video of another Black man, with a white woman falsely reporting that he was attacking her because according to him, he asked her to keep her dog on a leash in an area of the park where animals were not supposed to be unleashed.[d]

In the middle of this a friend sent me the Twitter (now X) hashtag *#BlackintheIvory* and asked me to read through the

---

[c] This Day in History May 25, 2020 "George Floyd is killed by a police officer, igniting historic protests" *History.com.* www.history.com/this-day-in-history/george-floyd-killed-by-police-officer

[d] Madeleine Aggeler. A Black Man Asked a White Woman to Leash Her Dog. She Called the Cops. *The Cut,* May 28, 2020 (updated) https://www.thecut.com/2020/05/amy-cooper-central-park-dog-video.html

threads. I stayed awake all night reading through those stories and I sobbed. My tears were both from empathy and from finally feeling seen, and from the realization that my experiences were more 'universal' than personal.

⋆⋆⋆⋆⋆

When I was subsequently invited to be a member of the strategic planning task force at the pharmacy school, I was the one who asked that diversity and inclusion be considered as a goal. I made this request at the time because more students of immigrant families were coming through our doors on their way to fulfilling their American dream of becoming pharmacists. If we succeeded in adding a diversity and inclusion goal to the strategic plan, I thought, perhaps there would be an impetus for making these students' experiences in our school something to write home about.

After the planning, came the implementation. I was tasked with chairing the committee/council for the diversity and inclusion goal. The first part of our task was to conduct a baseline campus climate survey. Working with members of the committee, we parsed through different surveys and by consensus decided on one available in the public domain. To prevent any perception of insider bias, I reached out to the company that conducted the climate survey we chose and asked if we could work with them. I made the arrangements and the administrative co-chair of the committee (a white male) assured me of budget approval and signed off on it. This was in the Fall of 2021.

What happened next was one of the most intriguing cases of administrative run-arounds I have ever encountered, with the administrative co-chair telling me we now had to turn the approval over to legal counsel if we were going to be publishing the results of the survey since students were involved. I reminded everyone involved that the survey was going to be anonymous and that the external company would have no idea who was answering what questions. Their role was to administer the survey on our behalf. In the middle of all this, I left for a six-month sabbatical and passed the baton to another colleague on the committee, hoping they would gain some traction on the survey while I was away. I returned to meet little to no progress on the work. What was meant to be a quick pulse survey to have been conducted in two weeks according to the company, kept getting pushed to a later date based on one excuse or the other from the administrative co-chair.

Little did I know that the recently minted university vice president of academic affairs (the former leader at our school) had shifted focus to a university-wide diversity program, instead of the work we were pursuing at the school level committee, knowledge my administrative co-chair was privy to. Yet, this man sat back and watched me expend precious energy chasing a project that he knew was not going to materialize.

A Leadership Change with Sidelining in Tow

The change in university leadership meant my school also had a change in leadership. The new leader (a white woman from Eastern Europe) had never shown any interest in diversity initiatives well before, and I surmised that the diversity goal was going to lose critical sponsorship. My concerns materialized even quicker than anticipated.

Our committee did not receive any level of administrative support from the new leader (she claimed that having an administrative co-chair on board was enough). Not only did she not support the work, but she also frowned at the committee's intention to use the public domain campus climate survey. And made a claim about concerns that the survey questions had been plagiarized. I responded to the email where she had expressed what I considered faux concerns, to let her know that I had permission to use the questions. She counter responded stating that she needed to see this permission in writing. (Was I irritated or what at the loud insinuation that I would use a survey instrument without permission?)

When this written permission was subsequently obtained, with the company stating that we could use the survey since it was in the public domain and we only needed to cite the source, this same supervisor said nothing and asked instead for a follow-up meeting as she did not want to keep lobbing emails back and forth. I on my part was left to wonder how she could go as far as insinuating that I was plagiarizing a survey meant to support the implementation of school-wide strategic plans.

THE BELONGING PARADOX

We had the follow-up meeting where she tried to convince me about her backroom support of our work, what with being the leader of the school. I told her I had seen the level of administrative effort and support afforded other school-wide committees. I let her know that she did not owe any of us on the committee anything by continuing to keep a goal on the strategic plan without fiscal and other support. I reminded her that strategic plans are dynamic and subject to change based on availability of resources and that she was welcome to write off this goal and assign us to other activities rather than having the committee expend time on this. She did not like my saying this, calling me rude and disrespectful and saying I was undermining her authority by telling her what to do. In this meeting, I witnessed my administrative co-chair so visibly disconcerted and shaky, perhaps due to being called into this, as witness.

After the meeting, I received a meeting summary in which my words had been completely distorted. Based on the emails that went back and forth with my asking for correction of this summary, it was clear that this was a deliberate attempt to miscategorize me and my work on the committee. Prior to this incident, all the committee work done under my leadership was being presented to the powers that be by the white male administrative co-chair. Someone I now realized that I had no idea how he was presenting the results, despite not having done any of the heavy lifting. The structure of this committee was representative of what many Black people I knew had experienced at some point or another. We did the grunt work and emotional labor, only for someone to take the results and present them in boardrooms where decisions about the work are being made, without us present.

I found myself invisible in the boardrooms where I sat over the course of my career in financial services.

It didn't matter that I graduated in the top 10% of my class in business school.
It didn't matter that I had excelled in all my roles, working at Fortune 500 companies. I was overlooked and didn't feel like I belonged

Why?
Because I was African?
Because my body looked different?
Because I spoke with an "accent?"
Because my hair wasn't "professional" enough?.
Because my style was too "eclectic.?"

I kept questioning myself.
Was I too much?
Did I need to blend in?
Should I tone it down so I could "belong"?

Then I had a realization that changed everything:

I WASN'T THE PROBLEM.

The biases were. The unspoken rules of "belonging" were. The outdated definition of what leadership should look and sound like was.
So, I stopped.
- I stopped shrinking myself to make others comfortable.
- I stopped dimming my light to match the room—I let my brilliance glow.

THE BELONGING PARADOX

> *- I leaned into my uniqueness, knowing it was my superpower, not a weakness.*
> *- I owned my voice, my expertise, and my right to be in the room; accent and all.*
>
> *And the moment I embraced who I was unapologetically, things changed.*
>
> *I learned that embracing who you were, would always be a winning formula.*
>
> *~ EM*

◆◆◆◆◆

I was no longer willing to continue playing these kinds of games. Moreso, because, when this co-chair had approached me to ask me to join him in championing diversity initiatives for the school, I made it clear that I was not there to do this work as a token. That I would take up the charge, only if assured of appropriate support from school leadership. He assured me I had nothing to worry about. But it became clear to me again that we had misaligned goals for this work, with him being in this for his own personal gains it seemed.

This was the same co-chair who when I indicated my intention to resign from the committee due to a lack of support, turned around to tell me that I was not as committed to the work as he would have liked me to be. That I appeared to be distracted by other things. To speak in Nigerian pidgin, I would have asked "Na which kain nonsense you dey yarn?"

But emotional labor came into play as I suppressed this urge and rather asked him to please remind me when me and him had any conversations about my outside work commitments that would lead him to make such an unfounded statement.[6] He apologized, stating that he misspoke. I responded telling him, I accepted this due and necessary apology.

THE BELONGING PARADOX

A Career Distraction and Belonging States

In the course of doing this diversity committee work, the new leader of our school denied my promotion to full professor, stating that I had led the committee for close to three years with no visible results. This statement was made even while knowing that I was away on sabbatical leave during this period and had handed over the work. Knowing that the reason for this denial was more than met the eyes based on my history with her, I appealed this denial decision with the university's leadership team and subsequently the grievance committee.

When she was called to testify about the case before the panel, she stated that the reason she denied my promotion was due to my lack of engagement. The women on the grievance panel (bless their hearts) asked her if faculty engagement was or had ever been a criterion for promotion, she said no. They asked her if she had ever spoken to me prior to writing the letter she used to support the denial decision. She replied stating she did not speak to me about her expectations (and definition) on appropriate faculty engagement. When the women pressed as to why she did not speak to me about this alleged low engagement being that she used it as a linchpin for her decision, she told them she had no reasons why and she did not know why she did not speak with me.

This was when I knew that we had crossed the so-called professional boundaries and that this was no longer about the work but more about how she felt about me as a person. Because my productivity and the quality of my work as an educator-scholar-researcher was a mile and more above other colleagues at the same rank whom she had vigorously supported, even in the face of glaring conflicts of interests, like writing "external" in support of their promotion even while serving as supervisor on record for tenure and promotion decisions. In my case then, rather than focus on the facts of the matter at hand and on my stellar work portfolio, she instead used so-called low engagement as a pretext for her denial of the promotion. This was now as personal as it could get, it seemed, to me (and some panel members who voiced concerns).

♦♦♦♦♦

The response my supervisor gave at the panel hearing, about not knowing why she did not do the right things by me, made me laugh at the sheer irony of it all. Because she was exhibiting what I have come to know as evocation—the concept that one's presence in a group can **evoke** certain behaviors in and from other people in the group that have nothing to do with anything we did or did not do.

Explaining Evocation

> *"The mere presence of a person in an environment alters that environment, independent of his or her traits and attitudes... even in the absence of any behavior at all. In evocation, the physical appearance of the individual unintentionally evokes behavior from others...behavior which, in turn, changes the situation for the evoking person. Evocation is ...exemplified by stereotyping and prejudice based on race, ethnicity and any other*

THE BELONGING PARADOX

social category that is marked by physical attributes. ...Indeed, many aspects of intergroup relations seem to involve evocation as a central mechanism. The mere presence of an out-group member in an environment populated by in-group members (or, for that matter, the reverse) can alter the environment by eliciting behavior from the in-group members that would not occur but for the presence of the out-group member."[7]

— John F. Kihlstrom

If you are one (like me) who is sensitive to cues in the environment. You may observe people's behaviors change, the more they get to know you and your brilliance, or when they see you not fitting into whatever categories they have placed you in their mind's eye. Recognize that what you may be experiencing is evocation. Your continued presence in their orbit evokes unconscious biases that can then manifest as overt or covert malicious behavior.

My supervisor had a history of not caring about my professional growth and trying to undermine my work. There were instances of me asking for simple accommodations, only to be met with non-approvals because according to her, she did not want to appear biased. Only for me to discover (by sheer serendipity) that even greater accommodations had been approved for others. When I would speak about my work, she would make remarks like "Everyone else can do this too", perhaps in attempts to diminish my work. I could speak about when she went and crossed out a submitted expense report by hand, and changed the amount to be reimbursed, because according to her, I had traveled over budget that one year. Never mind that this travel was to present my work (and represent the school) at national associations and receive leadership awards. Or do I speak to when she stated in writing that I was unprofessional, and that I was a plagiarist. Me saying that these were in writing is to say that I was privy to all these bordering-on-defamatory statements, and still have them in my possession. I could go on about my run-ins with this supervisor, but that would not be useful in the grand scheme of this narrative.

♦♦♦♦♦

While one could say, "Do not worry about such maliciousness and just keep shining", I do not make such flippant statements, because behaviors arising from evocation can be quite harmful, when taken to the extent of trying to wreck people's lives. For a leader to deny a well-deserved promotion, based on pretextual charges or prefabricated false equivalencies (like my supervisor did), borders on discrimination as described by the Equal Employment and Opportunity Commission (EEOC). In the US, the EEOC is the federal agency that prevents people in protected classes (like those based on race, gender and religion) from being treated unfairly on the job.

Evocation can also cause psychological harm, what with the constant overthinking about what and where one could have done things differently in certain situations. Not realizing that there was probably nothing one could do to satisfy people who are determined (consciously or not) to make life miserable for you as a person, (P) in their environment, (E).

To recognize a situation for what it is, is half the solution. Knowing that my non-belonging experience at work was probably due to evocation allowed me the freedom of thought and mind to keep doing my work and to limit my interactions with the individual(s) involved. To decide to limit interactions

THE BELONGING PARADOX

with such individuals at work is to be ready for the quandary of being labeled disengaged, or for false narratives to be spread about you. What a belonging paradox! Working on this book helped me tease apart the different sides of the paradoxical question of belonging at work for people like me and I hope that my writing about it helps you the reader as well.

♦♦♦♦♦

Recognize that evocation is not limited to adults. Children experience this too in certain environments. Which is why when Black people talk about institutionalized racism, please do not sneer at us, because you are not living our lives. I remember when my son had just moved to the school in our town. I had recently pulled him out of the Christian private school he was attending because I wanted him to expand his horizon and learn how to be in a bigger more complex school environment. He was in the third grade but was a whole year younger than other kids due to having completed kindergarten early. Cue to the summer after fifth grade when preparing for middle school. We were having a random chat about nothing when suddenly Child 1 piped up, "Mom, I have to tell you that when I first started in XXX elementary, all the kids were coming to me as the new kid, and they were trying to help me do things, but when they found I could hold my own, they all turned their backs on me." Oh! My poor child. And what might he have shown that he could hold his own on? His academic performance! This child has consistently been on the honor roll without fail in all the years he has been in school, winning prizes for academic excellence. A feat I cannot take any credit for. He does hold his own.

I found it funny that he would use the term "turned their backs on me." As an adult, I understood what he was trying to tell me. He had experienced a kind of prepubescent ostracism from kids who may have wondered how he could be so smart and capable since he was the new kid on the block, as well as being one of two Black kids in a class of 25 students. To think about it factually, if evocation can happen with a group of kids, why do we think that things would change in adulthood? The evoked behaviors may simply look different since adults no longer have playgrounds to keep friends away from playing with us, but the stakes can be so much higher.

✦✦✦✦✦

You may read about my work experience at my institution and think, "Well it is but a single story, of a single institution." I wish I could say the same but I have found the same types of behaviors based apparently on evocation, even in volunteer positions—on boards of nonprofits or working for the good Lord in church. It is not about the work environment or place. It is about the people in the environment. Even when the environment is foreign to us (as is the case with immigrants). It is the people in the new environment who extend warm hands of friendship and belonging that help make the new place feel a little more like home. This is why I cannot stop championing belonging as both something we can offer to ourselves and to others in any environment we find ourselves.

THE BELONGING PARADOX

Championing Differences and Found Not Wanting

My story does not end with my present or former colleagues and their actions or inactions. The beauty of work like mine is that I am able to act on my behalf. I have full agency. This recognition of my agency allows me to find ways to champion belonging for those in my space. And in my present workspace, that would include the students I interact with. While I am not a proponent of tasking individuals with trying to fix systemic issues, on the issue of belonging at work and in school, the work is personal for me.

Because I am different in many senses of the word, it is easier for me to see the things that many do not. When people have asked me why I have not left the job with all that happened, I echo hundreds of minority (although, I do not consider myself to be a minority in any sense of this word) women professors in many institutions around the country to say that; some of us do and did this work as some kind of vocational calling; there are too few of us in the professoriate; our presence in our classrooms serve as a beacon of what is possible. Students need to see that their dreams are as valid as those of us who stand and teach them how to enter (and belong) in the same professional spaces we presently occupy. Some consider this too great a task or burden to bear and I understand this sentiment. I get tired too. But for every day that I am able to help a student find their place in the professional world, I know I have done the Lord's work.

While one does not do work like this for accolades, it was gratifying to be the recipient of my institution's inaugural faculty award for student success and belonging. My narrative evidence of work done with students over the course of my teaching was the winning submission. Of the various awards meted out yearly at work, this was the one that most aligned with my values, one I also felt most qualified to receive. My goal was always for everyone who came into my classroom to know that they mattered and that I would do all within my power to ensure they succeeded, if they put in the requisite work. Now, with having to teach seventy, eighty young adults at a time, I will not always reach each one. Some may yet have unworthy things to say about me and my capabilities, but I know that for those I am able to reach, the ripple effects are long-lasting.

I feel called to the ones navigating many of those liminal spaces about which I write. Students (like me) from immigrant families who have to take care of their parents. Students who perceive themselves as not belonging. Students who feel that no one listens to them. For some reason, these students find me and I work with them. I try to walk them through the early years of discomfort before they find their footing. I do not want to walk with them for any longer than they need neither do I want to have to hold their hands all through their years in school. I just want to make sure their experiences in the early years are good and generative. There is nothing like self-determination; knowing you can achieve a goal and then getting to achieve those goals.[8] I know how it felt for me too the first few years on the job. I did not have anyone to model the way or anyone to call a [real] sponsor when I first started on the job.[9] Which invariably meant I had to find my own way. This was why the sudden exit of the former boss who I considered a mentor was so distressing when it happened.

THE BELONGING PARADOX

Many times, as I have seen with my own children, fostering a sense of safety and belonging in another person comes through listening. From my own experience, to know that one is heard or being heard makes all the difference. Therefore, I try to listen and listen well to people around me. To read and see beyond the lines of what they are telling me and to sit and be present with them.

> *I hear and see people in their mid-thirties, early forties, grappling with the same questions on work-based identity and belonging at work.*
>
> *As one very much vested in belonging practices, especially for young adults in, any messaging around belonging and finding your place in the world of work is even more pertinent to those just entering into the workforce.*
>
> *For many of these young adults, it may sometimes feel like entering into a world that is set in stone. Questions I want to be able to explore with them and help them find answers for themselves include:*
>
> *1. How do I find my place in the workplace?*
> *2. How do I navigate through various workspaces while staying true to my sense of self?*
> *3. What even is that sense of self? Do I know what it is?*
> *4. Will I be blown about by every wind that comes my way by way of different bosses and co-workers?*
>
> ### *Case in point:*
> *As an adjunct teaching and practice professor of organizational psychology, every year I have students in one of my courses write a case study. In this case they get to build the types of leadership development program they might offer as HR consultants. Each one of these students*

is in the workforce, either as an intern or junior human resources associate at different companies. Last year, for some reason they had a common theme in their projects that made a memorable impression on me (they told me they did not confer among themselves, and I took them at their word). All ten students highlighted leadership development programs centered around respect and communication and teaching bosses how to talk to their employees. Sitting through their presentations, I thought, "These young adults (ironically, they were all women), must be having such a hard time with being disrespected at work, for every one of them to have decided this was the thing that needed to be taught in the workplace."

During the project debrief, some made statements like, "Many times some of our bosses talk to us like we're not human beings". One of them said "I know I literally disobeyed my supervisor last week. She yelled at me in front of the customers I was attending to and told me to go to hell and go home. And I said, 'I'm not going home, I'm here to work. I'm being paid to work.' I walked away from her and continued working. I didn't even care, if they write me up for subordination. I was thinking, how could she talk to me like that in front of the customers and other staff and children who were there to be served." I responded saying, "I'm sorry you were treated that way. That must have been really hard." As she started to cry, she told me, "I'm so glad you understand."

While this was a temporary summer job for this student, I kept thinking what a missed opportunity as the young lady may never want to work with this organization again, despite, according to her, loving the job. All because her manager failed to signal belonging in what may have been a moment or day of frustration for that supervisor.

Belonging Corner Reflections

1) I write about the principle of procedural justice at work. Have you been on the receiving end of procedural injustices where different practices were applied to people in your workplace in what should have been otherwise standard practices? How did this add or take away from your sense of belonging at work?
2) What are some signals of belonging you have received from colleagues and others at work? Have you considered how you could beam signals of belonging out in big or small ways, to others at work?
3) If you think about instances of non-belonging you experienced and now realize how evocation might have played a role in your experiences, does it help you reframe your experiences in a different light? What would you do with this new knowledge as you continue to advance in your work and career?
4) For those on the neurodiversity spectrum, how do you practice keeping your sense of self in the presence of others at work who do not understand the diversity of human being-ness and experiences? How has trying to fit in and belong where you are felt for you? If you have been successful at fitting in, what were the practices that helped you?

PART IV

Belonging in the Faith

Stop trying to change reality by attempting to eliminate complexity.

—David Whyte

THE BELONGING PARADOX

From a cultural point of view, many of us are born into religious homes or societies where religion played a huge role in how our lives were constructed. Upon growing up and getting to choose our own ways, some of us walk away from the dictates of what we considered an orthodox way of being, while others of us walk toward what we consider the path of relationships and followership. We choose to walk in relationship with a monotheistic supreme being and consider ourselves followers of His way. The choice to walk into relationship is not only an otherworldly focused one, but we must also deal with relationships with newfound acclaimed brothers and sisters. These unspoken bonds of affiliation with other followers comes with its own belonging norms and challenges. How do we stay in relationship with others spiritually when our own earthly cultures and practices come with betraying tendencies? How does one belong in the faith?

Faith Spaces as Liminal Spaces.

I struggled with the decision to include the stories in this chapter. But belonging is both a broad (macro) and individual (micro) level concept. Our individual experiences of belonging cannot be discussed separately from the ways in which we mentally organize our experiences, and the meaning we make of them. Therefore, if I am to speak to the full experience of belonging in liminal spaces, then the faith or spirituality space as a life area must be a part of that mental organization for me.

Here, I will speak of my experience in the liminal space of being raised in a staunch Catholic home, and later becoming a Pentecostal Christian as my preferred faith expression (and identity) during my college years. Speaking of my Christian faith, it may be tempting to assume that commonly held beliefs about Christians in current society ("conservative", "evangelical", "religious", "right leaning" or whatever else people associate Christians with) apply to me. And I would laugh hard and long at that assumption, because one goal for writing this book was to highlight the breadth of human complexity. People are rarely as we assume, because of our propensity to see the world through our own frame of reference. The popular, sometimes misattributed quote "we see the world as we are and not as it is" bears this out. For example, my spouse, if asked, would probably tell you that he considers me a Christian egalitarian, one who believes in the equality of all men and women under Christ. While I certainly believe in Jesus and the canon of established doctrine, I also think too, for example, that a woman should have a say in how

THE BELONGING PARADOX

she wants to handle reproduction just as the man has his say in how he wants to handle birth control. I could go on about all the various assumptions and generalizations commonly held about Christian beliefs that I personally do not subscribe to. However, when all is said and done, I still hold on to a belief in a triune God.

A Believer and The Church

One reason I wrestled with this chapter is the deeply ingrained belief that discussing concerns about certain historic and current issues in the church amounts to criticism or a lack of love for my brothers and sisters in the Christian faith. My intention is quite the opposite. The first and greatest commandment for followers of Christ is that of love. A famous scriptural imperative regarding human error is for believers to "speak the truth in love". True biblical love should and does make no distinction based on gender, nationality, or ethnicity. In essence, all are welcome, and are invited to belong to the Church and body (of Christ) in every sense of the word.[a]

Growing up in Nigeria and now living in the USA for over 20 years, I have experienced the Church across two cultures and continents. Each has its own flavors in terms of how people are welcomed and socialized (both of which can impact an individual's sense of belonging). Before I dive into the rituals of fellowship and church attendance and how they serve to induct and socialize participants into church culture, I must establish certain foundational facts. It has been shown that involvement and participation in faith-centered communities confers several positive benefits on health and family life.[b] Some of these benefits could be attributed to the strong sense of community that accompanies being a part of a church. This

---

[a] Ephesians 4:15, New International Version,
[b] Jake Meador The Misunderstood Reason Millions of Americans Stopped Going to Church. *The Atlantic.* July 29, 2023.
www.theatlantic.com/ideas/archive/2023/07/christian-church-communitiy-participation-drop/674843/

THE BELONGING PARADOX

sense of community can be cross-generational/multi-generational. An additional benefit is that participating in faith communities can serve as a buffer for the seemingly unending social ills that are caused by a breakdown of social safety nets.

✦✦✦✦✦

For many then, church is where we go to find community and belonging. And we go with complete faith and trust believing that others are there seeking the same things. But the Church exists within the context of a larger society which means that churches more often (than not) reflect the values and mores of the society. Therefore, it is not altogether possible to separate church and state, as it appears that members bring their preformed beliefs, values and cultural ways of forming and maintaining relationships with them into church. For some, this can very quickly morph into a weekly ritual of attendance devoid of the type of fellowship, sharing of resources, and breaking of bread that was used to describe the first century followers of Christ.[c] Having spent nearly equal parts of my years as a Pentecostal Christian in Nigeria and the US, I will comment on belonging experiences drawn from my being a part of the church in these two geographical zones, each with its sociocultural characteristics.

Churches in Nigeria fall under the umbrella of the Christian Association of Nigeria (CAN), despite belonging to their own distinct denominations with different traditions, and forms of expression of liturgy and worship. One such distinct group was the Christian Pentecostal Fellowship with which many Pentecostal and nondenominational churches were

---

[c.] Acts 2:42–47, NIV

associated.[1] I give a little bit of this history to highlight that church in Nigeria was our unique African brand of Christianity, with plenty of imported beliefs mixed with our local cultures. Church in Nigeria with its unique combination of multiple denominations, and differences in doctrinal emphasis often led (regrettably) to the formation of different church camps based on sometimes zealous adherence to a particular brand of Pentecostalism.

♦ ♦ ♦ ♦ ♦

As a girl raised in the Catholic traditions, I had been steeped in the conservatism, and catechism of my faith, which included the practice of taking liturgical classes and asking questions. In college then, while most of my friends attended the trendy fellowships, I could not bring myself to join the groups of men and women in these spaces who (in my mind) went unsupervised and unchecked in comparison to the more orthodox congregations of my youth. I chose instead, to attend one of more conservative Christian fellowships on campus. From the proverbial view out of my window, these trendy fellowships were a huge marker of group belonging for those who attended them, as I observed from their interactions with each other. But I was still hesitant to join them. One of the primary reasons for my hesitation and my choice of a different fellowship from my friends was a seeming inability to shake off my growing degree of skepticism toward certain practices. One of these, the cultural practice of calling young men and women, pastors (and in later years, "Daddy and Mummy" or "Mama and Papa") and hanging onto every word that fell from their lips. This to me was in stark contrast with

THE BELONGING PARADOX

the biblical practices of calling other believers, "Brother" or "Sister", and of everyone searching the scriptures for themselves, while honoring people who had confirmed ministry gifts of teaching and preaching.

Therefore, I was only too glad to wave goodbye to the campus experience after graduation. Post college, I began attending a church where I held the no-nonsense founder high esteem based on his principled lifestyle. I was in that church for about five years before I eventually relocated to the United States. It was in that church I learned how to speak truth to power as a Christian and not turn the other way in the face of social ills like corruption. I learned how to be my brother's keeper indeed as we had an active clinic at the church where medical personnel could serve and I did so with joy. It was also in that church I discovered that one could in actual fact build community and develop a sense of belonging in a church that large by volunteering and serving. As it turned out, serving with other medical personnel in the clinic meant that my closest friends and associates at church were other health professionals, albeit with some diversity in terms of age, gender, marital status, language and ethnic origin (Nigeria has over 250 distinct ethnicities and 500 languages). There I was in such a large church, yet increasing the diversity of my friend groups.

In that season, within the context of this chapter, belonging in church was not something that one consciously thought about. Church was like home; it was where we went to get "plugged in" (recharged was the phrase we often used). We went on Sundays and to mid-week services, got recharged and went back into life outside. Additionally, the logistical and technological challenges in the broader Nigerian society did not allow time to dwell on what we were missing, not to speak then of the luxury of analyzing whether we belonged or not. I was all too happy to have found a church I could worship in, and be an integral member of the community. In terms of communal belonging, I had it at work, I had it with friends as well. Life was full and good as it generally ought to have been for an emerging adult trying to make their way in the world. Then came the mini earthquake event of becoming uprooted and dis-orientated through migration.

THE BELONGING PARADOX

Coming to Church in America

When I moved to the USA for my PhD, I quickly sought connection to a community of faith. I initially started out attending a predominantly Black American Church in Germantown Philadelphia because of its proximity to where I lived, but despite a warm welcome at a fellowship with people who looked like me, Sunday after Sunday, I struggled. It was difficult to understand the terminology (even though the services were conducted in English). While I received the welcome letters and giving envelopes in the mail like clockwork, I did not experience the type of boots-on-ground follow-ups and home visitations that I was exposed to, growing up in the Nigerian church community. Despite the seeming sincerity of the church leadership and members, it all felt very strange. At the time, I came to realize the impact that nationality and culture could have on expressions of faith and fellowship within our communities. So, it was the "church culture shock" that prompted my leaving to go find belonging elsewhere.

I moved to what one might call a "Nigerian church in the diaspora". An offshoot (church plant) of a very popular Nigerian denomination, it provided the many elements of cultural belonging that were particularly important to me in that season as a fresh migrant. It offered familiarity, community, and a way to stay connected to my home country. It felt like home, in terms of languages spoken, the meals we shared, and in the way the services and sermons were conducted. Then we moved to the South, and to a different type of church.

*****

I must continue here with an important caveat; what I write in the following sections are a summation of my varying personal experiences. It does not and cannot be extrapolated to assume that I am speaking on behalf of the entire church, or even of others who may have walked the same path and shared similar experiences. I speak only about my—sociocultural intertwined with geographic locations and people—experiences in various churches in America. Furthermore, what I write about these experiences may not align with what many have read or assumed about Christianity in the USA. As you will read later, my experience with belonging to various churches in America includes that of being part of a church community in the southern United States. And I can say without reservation that was one of the best church experiences I have had to date. And I say that unabashedly (or "with my full chest out" as we Nigerians like to say)

THE BELONGING PARADOX

Church in the South

It began with one simple choice. After eight years in the Nigerian church in Philadelphia, I agreed alongside my husband that if we were going to be living and working in America, (as we were), we needed to also make our Sundays an American experience too since church did not exist on its own outside of the society. We were also keenly aware that if we said we were Christians and we flocked only to people who looked like us, who spoke like us and talked like us, then how were we going to be able to do the work of going out into the world? Lastly, we thought that if truly the kingdom of heaven was going to be made up of people of every nation, tribe and tongue, then we (literally) wanted to see and experience what that looked like here on earth. And America being the melting pot of nationalities that it was, would be the one country on earth to experience that in.

Once the decision was made to search for a multiracial and multicultural church, the next singular factor was prayer. I prayed that God would lead me to a place filled with joy and love. Because with Christianity, as I sometimes saw it practiced back home, it could very easily become filled with laws and rules. What I came to know as legalism or "following the letter of the law" with more focus on form and process than on learning how to be a disciple of Christ and his teachings. I knew that love would see a person first before any other traits or characteristics. I knew that real joy at being in the house of God and around his people could not be faked (you only needed to look into eyes for cues), no matter what appearances looked like.

I went searching on the internet, of all places, and found that a certain itinerant gospel worship minister that I used to love listening to his songs in Nigeria had settled and planted a church in Nashville. I decided to guest sample the church and as soon as I walked into the premises and the building, I felt in my gut that this was going to be a new home for however long we would be in Tennessee.

THE BELONGING PARADOX

The Southern Winds of Church Community

Moving from the unending bustle of life in the Northeast to Franklin, Tennessee was like switching from a blender to a percolator. One of the first things I noticed about the South was that it truly was the "Bible Belt" (or more accurately, "church belt"). There appeared to be a church on every block. The number of churches in any square mile was quite remarkable, and was in my view a testament to American evangelicalism.

Life in the South was slower and friendlier. The friendliness and propensity to stop in the middle of whatever was happening and just chat took some getting used to for one was by now used to non-stop activity. This friendly culture permeated the church as well. I found the phrase "Southern hospitality" as culturally stereotypical as it was, to be true in a certain sense. The only difference in externals was that in the South, the racism was more overt compared with the Northeast. There was very little closet or covert racism. You could usually tell from the outset those who would rather not have anything to do with your type. So, you knew to stay away (if needed), or you tried to win them over with love and affection. As happened with our next-door neighbor, who came to welcome us on the day we were unpacking our truck, all while carrying a holstered gun on his hip (Tennessee is an open carry state).

Our family won him over with love, affection and Nigerian Jollof rice. In the end we became the very best of friends to him and his daughter. Such that this grown man, although he never did come to church with us, cried when we were moving away, telling us that he had never had such kind and openhearted neighbors. I always wondered what would have happened if we had met him with the same level of covert aggression he had approached us with that first day. Our experience with this neighbor served as a cogent reminder of the power of love applied in the context of our day-day lives as I have seen in action. Sadly, stories like this do not always work out that way; a different next-door neighbor never reciprocated our acts of neighborliness or friendship.

◆◆◆◆◆

What made church experience in the South so memorable? I believe it was the culture. My family experienced genuine affection and friendliness from people we attended church with. I did not encounter much pretentiousness. My son was welcomed fully into the amazing nursery and early childhood learning center. It was in that church I truly learned what it was to model going out into the streets and being the so-called hands and feet of Jesus. In addition to international missions work such as helping to prevent child and sex trafficking, serving the people in the church and the local community was baked into the church's mission and vision. And we all pitched in to accomplish the mission. Three examples focused on hospitality come to mind. I use these examples because as we will see, there is nothing like genuine hospitality to draw people in and make them feel at home and welcomed, even if one is not in a physical building.

1. We had a weekly food packing and service to the homeless experience, open to all members of the

church. We packed bags full of ready to eat foods that were then loaded into trucks and delivered to homeless citizens across the city. Being a part of this serving experience opened my eyes to the complexity of homelessness as a situation not easily remedied by building (or opening) more shelters. I learned that while the wheels of local and state governments turned ever so slowly, we could do our parts to ensure that people did not add hunger to the indignity of having to live without a roof over their heads.

2. We partnered with Sophia's Heart Foundation, a not-for-profit foundation dedicated to transitional housing for women and children living in poverty and working their way back from other adverse childhood experiences.[2] This was a women centered ministry but you could bring your kids (a belonging touchpoint for me as a mother). So, once a month I would take my son and we would cook and serve and eat with the residents of the center, some of whom had lived there for close to two years. No two families in this place were the same, just as none of their stories were the same.

3. The third experience was with what we called the hospitality ministry. This was a ministry devoted to any church member who had a baby or was experiencing some sort of familial stress that left them unable to take care of basic house functions like cooking and cleaning. Members of the hospitality team worked from a roster where we signed up to meet needs directly. We signed up based on our availability, distance to the church member, and meal or task preferences. I found myself getting to know people

more intimately as I went to drop home-cooked meals. I had a bias toward the new mothers on the roster because I knew how hard it was to take care of a newborn and still find time to cook good nutritious meals. Of course, I butted up against cultural differences. I remember my first home visits where I would deliver the food in my fine China the way we did back home, asking for them to be returned when they were done with the food. After one or two non-returns, I learned to use sizable Tupperware or aluminum foil pans to pack the meals (hilarious now, this presumption of shared values).

Was it easy being that I had a full-time job and a child of my own? Not in a million years, but serving in this ministry, along with my teammates, felt like what we were called to do. Especially being that no one, certainly speaking for myself, was coerced to do this for people we had no relationships with outside of attending the same church. To me, working in this team was another way to practice my faith as taught in scriptures — "If you do good only to those who can do good to you, what credit is that to you?"[d]

Working across these three areas in addition to serving in the church's full-service cafeteria as a runner and busgirl serving breakfast and brunch to guests coming into our church services was an enriching lived-faith experience.

---

[d] Luke 6: 33, NIV

THE BELONGING PARADOX

Clear Air Turbulence

Now, what could go wrong?, one might ask. Well, since church is made up of humans, (who do very human things), this church being no exception, we certainly observed boorish behaviors every now and then but at no time did we ever feel like this was a place for *"insert faction here"* only.

Incidentally, the one bump I came up against in our time there was with a Black Southern lady leading a marriage class at the time. My husband and I wanted to attend the classes to gain more insight into marriage teaching and education. Having just relocated, we had not found any local babysitters, so we showed up to the session with our 20-month-old in tow. Now, as was the tradition in many African societies, mothers with young children often carried their kids in a sling on their backs for convenience, so they could have their hands free for chores. So, when my husband and I showed up with our son slung on my back (wearing our fancy clothes), this sister did not appear at all pleased. She began by saying, it was a couples-only class and that it appeared they were not clear enough in the communication about whether children were allowed. She went on to further state that since my baby was a baby (obviously) and if he was not going to be disruptive, then perhaps we could stay if we wanted. I told her we wanted to stay. That we had seen the announcement for the small group and thought it was something we wanted to be a part of. I talked about how we were new in town without a sitter and we did not want that to be a deterrent to our participation.

With my baby sleeping peacefully in his back sling

♦♦♦♦♦

Another slight bump, still from this marriage class. Our host had been teaching about how as good Christian women we ought to let our husbands treat us like ladies and queens and that she tells younger wives to get into the habit of letting their husbands' open doors for them, including car doors. That ensuring this helps him know how to treat you well and that you also get used to being treated like a lady. I remember thinking "What?" How does this one singular act relate to gentlemanliness or be a sign of proper treatment? So, I raised my hand as I do when I hear teachings like this and I asked her

THE BELONGING PARADOX

a question. I said, "We have a child still in an infant seat and who needs to be prepped to get out of the car seat and into the baby stroller, which also needs to be brought out of the trunk and set up. Does a husband open the door for the wife who then goes ahead to do all those things or does he do all those things and then comes and opens the door for the wife? And while he is doing all those things, does the wife simply sit in the car like a child and wait for him, when she can open the door, get out of the car and help her husband since they are supposed to be a team."

It was clear that she did not appreciate my question as she continued insisting that ladies learn to let their husbands open doors for them. I did not intend to put her on the spot, although it may have felt like that at that minute. I simply wanted, through my questions, to bring up a different perspective as it was apparent in the course of class that she was speaking from the liberty of her season of life as an almost empty nester.

We, on the other hand, were there in that class, with one baby (and planning for another). The question I asked therefore was not illogical, given my background and culture of origin. To take a second look at the issue of opening car doors; I did not own a car until I was in my late twenties, at my very first job. I learned to drive by enlisting the help of friends and paid mechanics, since we did not have semblances of properly licensed driving schools at the time. Therefore, taking the realities of my life experiences, some of her recommendations for a good marriage did not make much sense. This "teaching" was not only impractical, but also appeared unbiblical to me, borne more from socioeconomic considerations. I would have had to inhabit a different body and consciousness to become the type of woman who would

Belonging in the Faith

sit in the car and wait for someone else to leave their side of the car and come and get me from my side.

Amidst all the positive experiences we had, this was one of those small reminders about unspoken codes of conduct which, if unexplained, can lead to feelings of non-belonging. For both us and this small group host, we had bumped up against "different." A whole lot of different, regarding customary behaviors, I would dare say. Here I was, a woman and mother, not only new to the church, but to the area and generally to the country, a woman who was not familiar with the genteelness of the people in the South.

✦✦✦✦✦

I have thought a great deal about that initial mismatch of expectations between that small group host and me. As a result, I decided to set out a separate section on belonging for individual parents in the community (see Belonging in Parenthood). Because our family felt overall welcomed and wanted in the large church, we were able to assimilate well into the church community and none of these minor incidents disrupted our sense of belonging in this space. But the story may be different for other families.

Speaking of family group belonging, private companies like all-inclusive resorts for example will state from the outset which of their resorts are either family friendly or adults (couples) only, so that any person wanting to visit or conduct business knows to set expectations. Churches many times do not (cannot) set these types of expectations by default, as that would defile their mission statements (and turn people off). This means that in these shared (sacred) spaces, implicitly open to all, people are supposed to come as they are. Many take up the invitation and come, but then bump up against unspoken norms and codes of conducts based on cultural ways of being.

With increased understanding of shared spaces within an individualistic society like America, I can realize that some of the onus is on me to ensure that others who are sharing a space with me are comfortable. The presence of my baby may have been discomfiting for some, who may be distracted by wondering if and when the baby was going to cry and cause an interruption to the teaching and therefore to their evening. I would also have to be mindful that not every couple in that space had children. Some may have been longing and praying for children and yet to see their prayers answered and thus, the presence of a baby might be an emotional trigger.

Having said that, I will say that is a lot of burden (of presumptive thinking) to place on a young mother with a baby who simply wants to fellowship with other believers. My perspective comes from being raised in a more sociocentric (collectivist) society. At church back home, we had children running about and in between parents' legs, while their parents engaged in what we called "fellowship after fellowship" conversations. Many churches catered to new moms with a nursing mothers' section at the back of the sanctuary where mothers could go if their babies fussed. To be in a place and to see other people in the same nursing season of life for many of the women must also have been a mental health booster as they saw they were not alone. To know that they could attend church, nurse while listening to the sermons, and not feel like they were a burden.

Our marriage class host then, from a belonging frame, should have welcomed us from a place of curiosity, asked about my back sling and then introduced us to the rest of the group. Then after the class, to sit or walk out with us while explaining the small group norms in an affable way. For her to have met us from this unspoken stance of "You broke a rule because the class is for couples only", was not a human-centered approach. Again, I say this a decade later only after much learning myself, while also recognizing that she might not have known any better about being an effective cross-cultural small-group host.

THE BELONGING PARADOX

Flying Back East

Asides minor bumps, we had a wonderful time doing ministry in that church. I was really sad to leave because I felt I was in the middle of building authentic community. But it was the Winter of 2014. Winds of change were starting to blow in, and it would be time to pick up sail again. We moved back to the Northeast in early Spring 2015 and began a new chapter of life and church.

There is an unfortunate (and sad) caveat to my blissful story of our experience with church life in Tennessee. We would come to learn a year later that the church leadership split and many members, many of them dear friends, ended up leaving the church. All because the senior pastor supported the US Republican Party's nominee in the 2016 presidential elections stating that he was going to be used by God to change the direction of the nation. We were not there to witness this in person and so cannot say what we would have done and how the church split would have impacted us and our belonging state. In the end, it showed me that you cannot divest church from society when things like political power and the impact on people's beliefs rub against the other. I have nothing against people's choices or beliefs, I only think though, that this pastor forgot the famous maxim *"No plan survives initial contact with the enemy."* He may have thought that because the church was deeply rooted in a 'red state', that all members of the church thought about politics in similar ways. We, on our own end, watched this turn of events from New Jersey and wondered what lay ahead for us and the Church in America in the coming years, whether north or south.

Migrating North: Northeasterly Church Winds

Our return back to the Northeast region set off a season of church itinerancy. We initially tried returning to a branch of the Nigerian church we were attending before we had kids but our children roundly told us that they did not want to attend this church, because it was too "Nigerian" in outlook. While we shook our heads in dismay at the concept of the kids already making a distinction between Nigerian and American churches, we understood the importance of ensuring kids were included in a church experience. We had always believed that church was not only about the adults and their preferences, that the kids deserved a voice too. We found a church online that appeared similar in form and function to the one we attended in Tennessee. We attended for about ten months and made a few friends but soon made the decision to look for a church closer home as this church was about a 40-minute drive away. I am a big believer (no pun intended) that one need not travel a day's journey to find a church community. Otherwise, it is no longer trying to find community in place but more about allegiance to a particular institution.

After three tries, we found a place close to home that fit our vision of what church should look like: multiethnic and nondenominational. But, as the saying goes, "Life is what happens to you when you're busy making other plans." A few months after walking (I use the word walking literally because we could walk the distance) into this church community, we bought our first house on the other side of town. And it

THE BELONGING PARADOX

appeared we were going to have to commute to church again. Thankfully, the church home we found had many campuses across the state. So, we were able to move both home and church by choosing to attend a different campus much closer to our new home.

After Christmas service, in our first home, circa 2016

Am I a True Jersey Christian Girl or Not?

The experience of diverse demographics in the area where one resides can hit differently based on one's socioeconomic status. This might appear obvious to some but it was surprising to discover that Northern New Jersey, a supposed bastion of multiculturalism and cultural diversity actually felt like little pockets of segregated townships. With each township being its own independent municipality with a mayor, public schools, fire departments, and emergency services, there was no pressing need for residents to go outside their towns for anything. We encountered many individuals and families who had lived in the same township for generations, with little exposure or ties to surrounding municipalities. We discovered tight-knit communities that had a fierce loyalty to their communities of origin, some of which went back generations. People born here were proud to be from here and let you know so at every turn.

These observations combined with our own more sociocentric ways and the extremely high cost of living made me wonder if I had made a mistake with the move down here for a job. But such is the immigrant experience. A life of movement. Of being on the lookout, ready to pack up, and to move to places where we can bring to pass a vision for a better life (for us and for our descendants). For so many of us, a better life also for members of our families back in our home countries who did or were not able to accompany us on our migration journeys for various reasons. To be a migrant, is to live in a state of liminality, because you are both "here" in the

THE BELONGING PARADOX

place you have chosen to live and work, and "there" in your commitment to your ancestral roots. Being a migrant is also by definition to be in a continuous process of assimilation.[3] Knowing that assimilation can be both a process (forced and quick, or progressive over time) and a choice, the choice to enter into a new country (and culture) implies that we have chosen to undergo some degree of assimilation. The process then, of further assimilation and integration, can be made easier by both the system, and the people living in the new culture.

✦✦✦✦✦

As it goes for easier societal assimilation, so it should go also, for church socialization, community building, and belonging. In my almost one decade of being an almost-North Jersey girl, I have found belonging to be both far-fetched and hard-won. Due to what I have come to describe as a unique Northeastern blend of in-group behaviors that is steeped into the fabric of life here. To not be born and bred in New Jersey is to be by definition an outsider. Nothing wrong with being an outsider. I mean the whole concept of the country as we now know it officially was based on outsiders coming into new territory and being initially welcomed with open arms.[4] What happened next is still up for historical debates and is beyond the scope of this book.

To be an "outsider" hoping to build cross-cultural relationships, but continually experiencing a pattern of being treated as an outsider is difficult enough to navigate in broader society. It is especially challenging to also encounter this within church walls, particularly since the Church—at least in my understanding of its original design—was meant to be a safe, welcoming and supportive environment for all, particularly the "outsider." Encountering the same kinds of in-group vs out, subtle or not so subtle exclusionary behavior here has been hard to wrestle with. In particular because we had as I wrote earlier, a very different experience in a church community, in a part of the country historically considered more racist.

Attempting to dismiss the behaviors I observed in another predominantly white church, this time in New Jersey, would require me to ignore the evidence before me. It would require me to ascribe it to something else, something about us as the outsiders, perhaps. What has been particularly hard to take in is the observation that within this partially multicultural community, the individuals that showed themselves to be true sisters and friends—rising and walking together in prayer and fellowship as the need arose—all happened to be Black, or of other ethnicities.

•••••

How did this happen? It certainly was not from want of trying to diversify our circles. Once in the church campus, we endeavored to find community at the local level, as had been our practice, by joining a small group. Many community circles in faith-based organizations are called life groups. And there's a reason for this. The goal is to "do life" in all its messy, wild and sweet ways, together. You cannot do life well with people if there is no corresponding sense of belonging. I had been in a functional and diverse group at the former church campus, meeting every week. But with the move to a different campus, I had to find another small group. The first one I tried joining presented me with a life lesson on how not to reject people. It also served as a leadership lesson for me on how to ensure clarity in the transfer of (global) institutional norms to the (unit) local level.

At the new church campus, I had reached out to the leader of a women's group, advertised as an open group welcoming all women no matter their age and life-stage. During our email and text communications (having learned now from my Tennessee experience), I asked if moms of young children were welcome to bring their kids if they were unable to find childcare for any reason. This leader assured me that it should not be an issue. I was surprised then to receive a lengthy email the following week advising me that the group was more geared for older women in their empty nesting phase of life, and that she no longer thought that the group would be a good fit for me. I thanked her for the email and let her know that I found the use of email for such disappointing news, unbecoming of a sister in Christ. I reminded her about how she had pursued me relentlessly to get me into the group roster through text and voicemail but now that she had unpleasant news, she resorted to delivering it by email. In hindsight, I know how hard it is to deliver news like this that places one in an unfavorable light. To her credit, this leader later called to apologize and to let me know she was new at this and was learning from her mistakes.

After this episode, I decided I was going to focus my search on groups catering specifically to moms (of young kids). This proved easier said than done. But as the saying goes, if you notice something, you have to be the person to do something about it. I ended up co-leading a small group, a subset of a larger group geared at moms with young children. I and my co-leader, a white woman, volunteered to lead a sub-group for working moms who wanted to meet in the evenings versus stay-at-home moms who had spaces on their schedules to meet during the day. Splitting the larger mom group up in this way to fit our different mommy schedules, was a good compromise for all. Everything was going well with this new group, I thought. Until it was not. And this particular challenge came out of the blues, it seemed to me at the time.

> Email: Monday 9/16/2019 4.20 PM
>
> Hi,
> Thanks for replying to XX's email. Our summer has been exciting and busy. We were hardly in town for all of August. About our group, I guess the signs were obvious although no one wanted to talk about it. It was great serving with you and I enjoyed the 2 years we did this. In my case, I think my values about having one-on-one fellowship and getting to know people better that way overrode the convenience of using zoom. As a churchgoer, that feeling of being seen and heard and validated is important to me having been through a week in a somewhat hostile environment at work. While I appreciated the convenience of meeting online, I felt like none of these precious women really knew or connected with me as an individual and I could no longer reconcile the two. I am okay and at peace with my decision because I realize that it may be hard for people to change their social dynamics even within a faith-based (Christian) setting. And having lived in America for 14 years, I get it. At the same time, I am not able to continue to be in a space where you feel like the "other". This has nothing to do with you and more about me but I thought to let you know since you were such a great leader. I will see you around one of these Sundays. I trust work is going great. I learned a lot about how to act administratively from you and I know those skills will come in handy someday.
> Blessings,
> Otito

Notice the date stamp? Prior to 2020, I was quite reluctant to have virtual meetings as I thought they deprived one of relative face-to-face fellowshipping. Little did I know that COVID-19 and the subsequent shutdown of social activities six months later would come and do us all in where the only source of interaction with people at work and elsewhere was through virtual video meetings.

◆◆◆◆◆

The matter at hand that led to me writing this email was not really about zoom or virtual meetings. It was more about the connections made (or not made), and the visceral feeling of knowing if you were indeed a part of a group and that you were not together with others based on convenience. You see, we had been meeting for over a year, my co-leader and I, facilitating this small group alternately between our two homes. As working moms of two boys of about the same ages, I felt like we got along very well together, seeing we also served together so well in church. Hence our mutual decision to co-host and see what it looked like.

We began meeting officially in the Spring of 2017 with a plan to meet in person twice a month. Which meant that each of us only had to deal with hosting once a month. However, every time we met in my house, the co-leader and most other guests would go on interminably (it seemed to me) about how much food I had set up. They would ask questions like, "How on earth are you able to manage this as a working mom with two young kids at home?" I would go on to assure them repeatedly that feasting and fellowship was a part of life growing up in Africa. That, if it ever became a problem for me to host, they would walk into the house and I would have only ice-cold water as the barest minimum, as Jesus commanded us to do. And we would all laugh about it.

But after a while, I began to wonder if I was the one doing something wrong by making these women feel like they could not meet up to my hosting standards. It was quite the conundrum for me since I truly loved hosting people (hospitality is a key value for me). I ended up speaking with a senior mentor friend who advised me to read the room. She advised that while it might go against the grain of my worldview, that maybe I did need to consider minimizing the table spread and food options. This, she said, was to be done in the spirit of accommodation, (to make my guests comfortable seeing as they may have been expressing some level of discomfort by their statements) and not because I considered it bowing to cultural pressure.

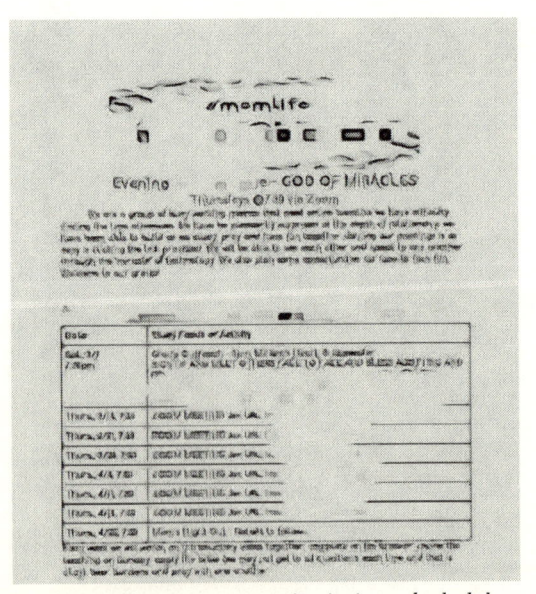

A virtual mom group meeting invite and schedule

THE BELONGING PARADOX

The opportunity to do this never arose because my co-leader subsequently suggested hosting virtual meetings instead. I told her that while my vision for leading a small group was based on in-person meetings, I would nevertheless try it out and see. Our pilot meetings went well, surprisingly enough. We had many more women join us than we could ever have had in person. In that respect, we could actually say mission accomplished. However, I observed two very strange things with the passing of time in this virtual meeting set-up.

1. My co-leader had given a lack of prep-time as her primary reason for moving the meeting online. A woman who had told me she had no bandwidth to host and meet in person began flooding my timeline (as a friend on social media) with pictures of her hosting weekly direct sales marketing events in her house.
2. The women that we were together online would see me in church and appear to have no recollection of me whatsoever. I was having to constantly remind so many of these women that I was with them last week online in our Bible study group. Then would follow the corresponding "Oohs" and the "I'm so sorrys." This happened so frequently that I stopped trying to say hello to many of them in church on Sundays. And I thought, "What type of small group was I leading and a part of, if I could not catch up with members of the group in larger church on Sundays?"

During my early career years, I joined a medical group where I happened to be both the youngest doctor and only Black woman in the group. It felt like I was joining a group of brothers and sisters as we all worked really well together, or so I thought. About three years into my time with this group, I saw on social media that one of my colleagues got married and had invited pretty much everyone in the group except me. Although this wedding was out of town, and I had young children and my colleague may have thought that I might not have been able to attend, however, the fact that I was not included in the conversation regarding the wedding made me feel very excluded and left out. I felt unseen. As someone already struggling with self-doubt this incident made me question myself even more as I kept wondering if there was something wrong with me.

Even though I come from a multicultural background where we are quite inclusive of people from other cultures.

After this incident, I resolved and I have tried to be as inclusive as possible in my interactions with other people, no matter who they are.

~AJ

THE BELONGING PARADOX

Am I Invited to The Party?

The final icing on the cake for me, in terms of belonging in this mom's group came soon after. My co-leader had a big birthday bash. And I got to see and read about it on social media. My decision to step down after this incident was one that I wrestled with for months. I sought the counsel of wise senior friends, both male and female, in order to get a balanced, thorough perspective. Hence my lasting six more months in the group.

Do I hear you thinking, "What's the big deal?" "People have birthday parties all the time and not everyone can be invited. This is not kindergarten." And I say yes to all that. However, when you see other members of the group you are leading, who you saw your co-leader get acquainted with only through facilitating the group, seeing as you both led the group; when you see many of these white women at the party, one that you knew nothing about, not even a word or whisper through all the months of planning and executing what appeared to be a beautiful party. I do not know about you, but I was transported back to elementary and middle school. A journey back in time, to be painfully reminded of cool cliques and groups versus not-so-cool others.

This was not just about being invited or not, but as I saw it, for your co-leader to not see you as part of the group you are both leading, to not consider it a thing to let you know their birthday was coming and that they planned to celebrate this fabulous birthday felt like being on the outermost fringes of a non-existent friend circle. The final result of this was me eventually emailing my co-leader and letting her know I would not be co-leading anymore. I told her she was not under any contractual fellowship bonds just because we attended the same church. Finis! We are still Facebook friends and still chat each other up every once in a while believe it or not. I am very aware that I earlier wrote about my telling another leader to be courageous and not give undesirable news by email. Yet here I was sending an email about stepping down from co-leading. It was not from lack of trying to meet in person, and I did not want to do this by text messaging.

THE BELONGING PARADOX

Separate and Together in Church

Like I stated earlier in my story, the main issue was not that the church group went virtual or not. Nor was it simply the sense of rejection from not being invited to a party. It was the gradual accrual of small, hurtful, and sometimes degrading interactions with some white folks. These encounters were all the more hurtful because they occurred within the church and in a region of the country that historically has held itself out to be more enlightened and therefore less racist by definition. Another belonging paradox.

This is in no way to say that all my small group experiences were negative. During the COVID-19 lockdown period in 2021, I happened to join another small group, albeit a little reluctantly. I joined because it was billed as a support group for those who were experiencing or had experienced racial trauma after the unsettling and very public racist incidents that occurred the previous summer. The incidents that summer ripped off the scabs that barely covered the discrimination wounds I had been facing at work but had chosen to ignore because I told myself I would not ascribe racially based interpretations to them. To then read online incidents about the experiences of other Black academics like me, trying to do their work but who experienced horrible discrimination, broke me and my fledgling faith in the meritocracy of the US system.[5]

•••••

So yes, I did need healing, from racial trauma, I reckoned. I went ahead and joined this small group with a structured, facilitator-led setting to discuss the book, *Healing Racial Trauma* by Sheila Wise Rowe.[6] Ms. Rowe was a Christian and professional counselor who had lived in and outside the United States. She had been a lay pastor for many years in South Africa, another country healing from the effects of a peculiar brand of racism and segregation called apartheid. As a Nigerian born girl who lived and went to school with many Black South African and Namibian refugees displaced by the racial conflict happening in that country in the aughts. As one who ran out into the streets to dance and sing songs by the South African Queens of Soul —Yvonne Chaka Chaka and Miriam Makeba—both when Nelson Mandela (Madiba), was freed and when apartheid officially ended with his election as the first Democratic Black President, I thought Sheila was likely to have a more nuanced view of the effects of centuries-old subjugation and the systems built under such ruling powers.[7]

⋆⋆⋆⋆⋆

Engaging with six of my fellow Christian sisters, who all happened to be Black, we read through Sheila Rowe's book. This reading changed me in so many ways, as an immigrant woman living in the Northeast. Processing this book communally with others allowed me to look inwards, to go within a body that was keeping score, and access and acknowledge the trauma (with a small t) that comes from certain forms of displacement. To recognize that immigration, as voluntary as it was for me, when met with exclusionary intergroup relations, represented what I have now come to know as "mini earthquake events" that can add to one's sense of displacement, disorientation, and lack of belonging.

THE BELONGING PARADOX

Naming, processing and acknowledging all this through lament was part of the work that we did as we worked through the many chapters in the book. I saw that in the Bible, God was not unfamiliar with displacement and slavery. He promised to be an anchor and a deliverer through the big 'D' and small 'd' displacements that come with living in a foreign land.

The Small Groups: In-Groups and Out-Groups

Based on this and other deeply personal experiences, a question then might be "What makes people feel like they truly belong within a faith-based group?" A group like the one with my co-leader, (who also happened to be a white woman).

Church hurt and the attendant feelings of betrayed trust and non-belonging are not unique to the immigrant experience or to me as a Black woman. I have watched many white people leave church for multiple reasons. As I stated at the beginning, this is not a book about church bashing. My goal is to help you restore your sense of belonging, and be able to do that from a place of centeredness, independent of others' approval or acceptance of you. Because God accepts us, as we are, on our way to becoming who we were designed to be. That humans are sometimes incapable of accepting us fully is not because there is anything wrong with you or me. I have come to realize that for many people, their inability to love the stranger is not always due to hatred of the stranger. It is about both capacity and ability. People cannot (are unable to) give things that they do not have.

> *God loves us and is accepting of us. That humans are sometimes incapable of doing this is not because there is anything wrong with you or me.*

THE BELONGING PARADOX

✦✦✦✦✦

In the field, and social psychology of intergroup relations, it has been shown that a person's attachment to their preferred social group (in-group) is not always correlated with hatred toward other out-groups. Research has shown that the bias and group preferential treatment we observe is not always due to direct hostility toward other groups but rather an offshoot of people's preferred treatment of members of their in-groups.[8] Just like in the case of the party invite. I believe my co-leader invited those who were similar to her, people she preferred to party and have a good time with, and the outcome of that preference was what I observed.

We are humans with preferences. We like what we like, and we like who we like.[9] As much as it hurts my fingers to even type that, it is an obvious truth, even if one refuses to acknowledge it. And if there's anything I am committed to, it is a search for truth and to tell it as I know it. As Christians, sometimes we (I must also not exclude myself) like to ignore the evidence before us. The imperative that was given to us was to love. It does not necessarily mean to 'like' or 'fawn'. Love is found in deeds and in actions and not in sitting around feeling cozy, while sending thoughts and prayers. Loving others might mean making a commitment to check in once weekly or to do some other tangible acts, **in addition** to those thoughts and prayers.

Church Notes: Doing Belonging Well at All Levels

I still live in the Northeast presently, and participate in church life here. While the stories in this section showcased a few challenging belonging experiences, they again were not intended as an exercise in "church bashing." There are way too many good things found within the Church to simply surrender to grievance and walk away from it all.

◆◆◆◆◆

> *Many folks like me are searching for something; some measure of assurance, stability and community in a world that has lost many of the social reinforcements that held us up symbiotically in times past. Call me naive but I still believe that church when done well can bring some of that back. Key words are **if** and **when** (done well).*
>
> *The commandments to those of us in the church, to welcome strangers, to do good to those who hate us, to turn the other cheek, to walk an extra mile with a brother or sister...I imagine a world where we did that simply for the sake of the Word and not power or political gains. This is probably harder now to imagine than ever before. But that is not to say we cannot do the right thing at the individual level by opening up our arms and helping people belong. And in turn teaching others how to practice true hospitality free of cultural pressures.*
>
> *We can do this in creative ways as best as we can within the society(ies) we find ourselves in. This will not be easy work; showing*

> *love (and belonging) in both words and deeds, but it is and must be necessary ground level work.*
>
> *Part of this work will include teaching people about inter-group relations and cross-cultural communications. Doing the foundational work to foster belonging in the faith is going to require different mindsets and systems. Because as the Church, we have been called to an overarching (or superordinate) goal. And that goal is to embody unity and harmonious co-existence as one body in Christ, even with different parts serving different functions.*[e]
>
> *In my work in facilitating Cultural Intelligence workshops, the greatest concern participants have is always about having to change who they are just to make others comfortable. And as facilitators, we are required to remind them that becoming more adaptable culturally has nothing to do with changing the essence of who they are. We can all increase our knowledge of others' cultures and ways of being. This in view of enabling members of the body to be ready to welcome any stranger in our midst at all times.*
>
> *Doing belonging well is also not work to be done only at the 'corporate' pastoral level. Individuals have to be equipped with proficiencies to be able to do this at every level, especially at the small group or fellowship circle levels. As the Church, we should not require that people adapt and assimilate to our ways in order to find belonging.*

Some may consider the act of finding and fostering belonging in church a luck of the draw. I do not believe that it is. Enabling true belonging in the faith is a foreshadow of how

---

[e] 1 Corinthians 12: 12-13, NIV.

things can be when we set aside all things that can separate and divide, and try our best to come together as one to fulfill our missional work. The next sections are devoted to the 'How to' of enabling belonging. In them I cover ways and practices to foster belonging for ourselves and others. We will learn about how small everyday interventions that do not require much (capital or resources) can change the narrative of belonging for many people. Putting them into practice, will require learning to lead from the heart, not the head.

Belonging Corner Reflections

1) Have you ever had your belonging questioned in a place of worship? How did this make you feel when we consider that church is meant to be a place where there is neither Jew nor Greek, master nor slave, a place where everyone is supposed to be welcomed regardless of class, circumstances of birth or social status?
2) Do you think your culture, be it national, family or personal, has played a role in how you view and treat your brothers and sisters in Christ? Is there any way in which you think you may have failed to signal belonging to your brothers and sisters at any point in time in your faith journey? If so, what practical knowledge and practices are you applying to ensure that you are loving your neighbor into higher levels of state belonging at the minimum?
3) How do you think you can contribute at the group level to making others belong within the body of Christ, recognizing that we all come with different personalities and ways of being? How do you ensure that you are not indirectly enforcing assimilation on your brothers and sisters of different cultures through unspoken norms and beliefs that you may be holding them accountable for?
4) How can you practice integration and wholeness as a person of faith by beaming belonging signals out into the world to be seen as love and light? What courageous conversations and acts of commission are you willing to engage in as you work with those who are from a different group than you?

PART V

Belonging in Parenthood

When people reject our children, they reject us as their parents too, even if they did not mean to.

—Author

Have you ever, as a parent, had a good friend come into a text chat group with a peculiar form of parental distress? An emotional state you recognize because you too have experienced it. This peculiar distress and frank helplessness is the kind a parent like me feels when the precocious intelligent child they raised, enters a modern-day kindergarten classroom and in the very first week and month, begins to receive reports about the child and their unsuitability for the shared school environment. It was this distress repeatedly witnessed over time in moms in my friends' circles that birthed the writing on these pages, where I focus now on the price of belonging, not as a child but as a parent of a child with different needs. A high enough cost as it were, further compounded by experiences within the larger fabric of a society that leaves no room for children like ours. What can we do to belong well as we continue to advocate for our precious sons and daughters?

Diversity Across Generations

I presently parent two amazing young men who entered my life and dismantled every single stereotype I had about how to raise boys. I will always be grateful for them, because in trying to work through my own confusion at what I at the time termed their heightened sensitivity, I had to learn both how to name my own feelings and how to talk them through theirs. I had to learn how to be comfortable with their tears, their big feelings, and their even bigger emotions. All of this, well before I knew these as signs of neurodivergence.

My Child 1 began talking way before he could walk and I basked in the wonder of parenting such a precocious child. Until some of the wonder waned. Because the other side of being the parent at home with him translated to not having enough stretches of quiet time for me who thrived on solitude (introverts, anyone?). It also meant life was literally turned over and up. As much I loved conversing and having adult conversations with him as a baby, sometimes I simply needed quiet brain space. So, recently when I heard one of the women in a special needs mom group recently confess that all she wanted was a few moments of quiet and respite from the ever-constant chattering of her child, it was a sentiment I too was familiar with.

As I leaned into Child 1 and his garrulous and loving nature, I remembered that I too was cut from the same generational cloth. I was the same child who constantly received the "Talks too much" and "Could be better organized" on school report cards in school. I look back now and think about how frustrating that might have been for some of my teachers.

THE BELONGING PARADOX

These moments of introspection served as a reminder of how much Child 1 behaved like me as a child. And that my irritation at his talkativeness was perhaps a mirror of the internalized unacceptance of my own chattiness as a child.

This realization led to promising my parenting self that I would not be the reason that my child loses his voice. I needed to teach him how to use that voice well as it was part of who he was born to be. Is he loud? Yes, when he wants to be. But he knows enough now about reading rooms to know those spaces where he can truly be himself. I made this seemingly insignificant parenting promise because I 'lost' my voice as a child from all the monitoring and externally oriented corrections for social propriety. I did in fact become less chatty so I could fit in.

With this same child, I learned to be more physically expressive. With him I learned how to receive and give hugs, something that both my upbringing and adverse childhood experience had made me averse to. Today, I am a hugger by way of my Child 1 and my life is the better for it. Because I learned to be fully wrapped and embraced in my child's hugs, I can in turn offer that gift to a hurting parent or child in return. I no longer have to explain that I do not do hugs. I now give hugs freely, both as affirmations and belonging signals for those open to it.

♦♦♦♦♦

The story of my Child 2 in contrast is the underbelly of my parenting life journey. From when he was about a year old, I sensed a heightened anxious attachment to me. I do not know if one could link this to the traumatic incidents surrounding his birth where I returned to the hospital without him for four days due to postpartum complications from an indifferent-to-Black-maternal-health care system. Or to the time when he spent three days in the hospital due to viral pneumonia and I could not be there with him because I just started a new job, and I had an older child to shuttle to school and back. There are many days when I feel like my absence during these crucial maternal bonding moments were a failure in parenting.

THE BELONGING PARADOX

Going to School from Home

In what some have called the price of upward mobility, many immigrants, our family included, learned about social dynamics of residential zip codes and schools. We learned that if you wanted your children in well-resourced schools, it might mean needing to live in predominantly white neighborhoods. Which in turn meant our children attending schools that were not demographically or ethnically diverse. A real circular dependency.

With this tacit knowledge for me, came the resulting ambiguity when incident reports from school came home with my child. As their parent I am more prone than not to think: "Is my child being singled out because they are different?" "Did what was reported to me actually happen?", seeing as my child is telling me a different story (never mind that children are sometimes inclined to lie because no one really wants to admit they are at fault). In addition to questioning my reality, various interactions with school personnel combined to engender so much "Mom guilt" and "Parental shame." Emotions that fueled feelings of not being enough as a working parent. Feelings that spiral into not feeling at home in a country one currently calls theirs.

This was eventually why I decided to end with stories and reflections on parental belonging to let parents like me know that we can make it. With the right orientation around place belonging, we help our children see that they belong. When we stand in our own belonging, we give our children, as they grow, permission to take up their own space and place. And hopefully, it would be more spaces of ease than we ever had to maneuver.

> On Thu, May 5, 2022, at 7:15 AM
> Otito Frances Iwuchukwu <xxxxxx@xxx.xxx> wrote:
>
> Dear Ms. Z,
>
> Happy Teachers Appreciation week (from one teacher to another). Thank you for all you do every day to ensure our kids are learning.
>
> I am writing to inform you about an interaction that took place yesterday between myself and Child 2 when I picked him up.... This was interesting to me because it's one of the few times that he has given me feedback unsolicited.
>
> It's my earnest hope that this will not be used as evidence against him. I just wanted you to realize that his vivid and sometimes over the moon descriptions of events can go both ways.
>
> Me: Child 2, how was your day?
>
> Child 2: I'm hungry and I'm not going to eat any more snacks at school.
>
> Me: Why, what happened?
>
> Child 2: Well, today I received a lecture from my teacher about how I eat snacks that are full of horrible ingredients like sugar, sugar, sugar. That the stuff I eat is absolutely horrible. And how she packs healthy foods for her children like apples, carrots, sandwiches, full meals and they didn't even have to get school lunch. She also said she understands

if we cannot afford the healthy foods because they're expensive in this country.

Child 2: My question Mom is; If the school is providing it for us, then how can she call it horrible?
Mom I am also the only one she lectures about food. She lectures others about beat boxes, about standing up, and about talking too much but I'm the only one she gave a stern lecture about my food and how I eat too much of the school meals. (End of story).

Again, please note that I am only relaying exactly what he told me last night.

While I am aware that many people tend to tie food choices with attention deficit issues and other things, I am also acutely aware about the implicit class divide that operates around food and food choices in America, be it intended or not.

While the motives may be right, the delivery and the attitude behind it is typically the issue.

I am not here to say this is right or wrong. I just think that for a child to have remembered this lone incident of all the possibly numerous incidents that happen in school every day speaks for something.

As an editor, the ethos and mantra I apply to my work and life is; Words matter, whether spoken or written. As people entrusted with the lives of the next generation to mold and to empower, it becomes more of an imperative that we use our words to encourage and that the words people remember from us would not be critical voices, criticizing their behavior and their food choices and whatever else we tend to criticize others for in this country (which happens to be far greater things than things we find to encourage them for).

So, if the scenario painted above actually happened then I have two concerns...

1. That a child was actually spoken to about affordability of food being that he has no frame of reference for comparison about what that affordability might mean.

2. We are already dealing with a child who tends to catastrophize unduly. I do not want stuff like this to lead him down a garden path of even more anxious thoughts in which he starts to think that his parents can no longer afford to feed him.

Because we may have our issues as many families tend to have, but affordability of food (healthy or not) is by the grace of God, not one of them.

That I am even having to write this note in a country that is ranked among the richest in the world, to me is a problem. School food programs and choices should not be part of conversations surrounding learning. But they are, in hundreds of classrooms around the country and perhaps we need to reflect more about why certain children cannot afford food even when their parents are working, full-time, sometimes multiple jobs too.

Thank you

THE BELONGING PARADOX

> Date: Thursday, May 5, 2022, at 11:17 AM
> To: Otito Frances Iwuchukwu
> Cc: J.J. H.H, O.O
> Subject: [External]Re: A Note About Food and its presence or absence in the classroom
>
> *Thanks for sharing! Although he was right about me having a conversation with him about food yesterday, it was not entirely the conversation. He has been complaining about being hungry all day at school. Yesterday he opened 5 cereal packages in addition to his lunch. I told him to ask you to please pack him food that will sustain him throughout the day because the cereal is loaded with sugar and although it is something to eat, it's the reason why he's still hungry throughout the day. He told me you're too busy to pack him lunch, so I told him that although teachers are very busy people, we can all find time to do that. Hence, what I explained I pack my kids each day for lunch. We didn't discuss financial difficulties at home but that schools can't afford to send kids healthy meals because it's too expensive. Although the conversation began with him, I did address the entire class as a few students complain often throughout the day of being hungry. However, most parents are not sending their children snacks or additional food. I will say as a parent who has a child with difficulties focusing in school, I have spoken to numerous specialists and performed research for the past 5 years and 1 thing that is certain is that sugar is the enemy for issues related to attention. It's the reason why I pack my children very specific lunches with protein/carb combinations and plenty of vegetables. I also have a child with nut allergies as I told the students which is also why I pack their lunch each day rather than allowing them to eat school lunch. I apologize if the message he received sounded accusatory or more like a "lecture." It was not my intent but rather motivation to help him remember to have a discussion with you when he got home. Please feel free to reach out to me with any questions.*
>
> *Stay well!*

This email thread was between me and Child 2's second grade teacher. I do not want to clutter this book with the sheer amount of correspondence that has been exchanged with school personnel, about this child. All I can say is welcome. Welcome to my world and to a slice of my interactions with some of the teachers in the public school system, as a parent of a child with "different" needs. Even my having to write about public schools is a symptom to me of a class divide. Because when speaking of social contracts, as a working parent and taxpayer, it stands to reason that if I am going to send my child to schools funded by those taxes, I would want them in top-rated schools, in terms of ensuring their physical, social, and emotional learning.

With children like mine, the question of school choice is no longer an easy one, but rather one laden with concerns for the child's fate. Do I send them to a school that crushes their self-confidence daily simply because I am paying taxes to the system? Or do I pull them out and homeschool them, taking a hit to the family income for the sake of their future? Questions with no simple answers. Questions that turn out to be questions of place, and of belonging for the child (and the parent).

THE BELONGING PARADOX

ADHD is Awesome. Or is It?

When you hear of children with problems focusing at school, children with special needs, differently abled children, or children on the spectrum, what comes to mind? Hopefully you do not have any one stereotype in mind because the huge diversity in learning and developmental abilities makes it hard to navigate this space. The story of my Child 2 bears this out.

When Child 2 entered kindergarten, it was not long before I began receiving daily complaints about his inability to sit still and him being a distraction to the teacher, what with him being too advanced for the class in all learning areas. Each report kicked my parental advocacy skills into overdrive, even as the school psychologist kept pressing us for a neuro-developmental evaluation. We met with a child study team who provided tips for us and his teachers to work cooperatively and advance his learning. Because, one thing was clear, the child disliked the school environment and called it exponentially boring. The pandemic lockdown of 2020 through 2021 provided a measure of relief from the school pressures. By this time, based on all the reading and research I had done, I was pretty certain the child was showing classic signs of attention deficit disorder. When we finally went for an evaluation, the diagnosis was confirmed and the school finally had something they could work with.

By this time, due to the incessant back and forth with the school system, I was more than ready for a change of place, pace, and perspective. Having already applied for a sabbatical at work, I unenrolled the boys from school and went back home to Nigeria. Although home was in the United States, I longed for my ancestral home. I wanted nothing more than just to be back among my own kin folk. While many of my friends and relatives wondered at the risk of taking two American-born children back to Nigeria for school, I knew I only had this one window of time. I wanted to show my children how school was done in a place where they were respected and affirmed for who they were.

A different School Experience: At London Heathrow airport waiting for our transfer flight to Lagos

THE BELONGING PARADOX

In Nigeria, Child 2 tested into a grade above his grade back in America. In the 16-weeks they attended school for the first term of the year, I did not receive a single call from any of the teachers, or the nurses, or the various headteachers. The teachers did let me know during the scheduled mid-term parent teacher meetings that he still had his big emotions at the slightest issues but assured me that they had it under control. The nurses told me categorically that part of their responsibility at school was to be a reflection to parents of having a village to take care of your child and that I would be called or alerted if there was a very serious issue. The peace of mind I had regarding school choice was priceless. When it was time to return to America, the child told me that although it had been hard at first because the teachers were so much stricter, he was still thankful that we made the trip.

Upon our return to America and school, we met a different school principal. Armed with an official diagnosis based on all the neurodevelopmental evaluations we did; I went on to ask for school accommodations. I took this action based on advice from other parent-friends of ours who were also navigating the system of special needs and school choices.

The new principal assured us that having ADHD was not the end of the world and that they would do all in their power to help Child 2 out. About a year later, the school psychologist resigned abruptly in the middle of the year. We had to navigate the system all over again with a new psychologist. The same teacher from second grade who had given us all that hassle had moved to teaching fourth grade and asked for a second chance with him. She told me she wanted to help bring some sense of stability, having seen that change was hard for him. We agreed and the year passed quickly. One year and the next grade later, and we had him with a male teacher. A teacher my child adored. A teacher who saw him for his abilities and potential and worked really hard to help him.

I will confess here that I lay down on many nights and wonder why it had to take a male teacher to see the child and to help him without any measure of judgment. As a mother and educator, I know what it feels like to be seen and heard, and to be given the space to blossom with proper guidance and direction. In my heart, I wonder why other mothers (as teachers) were unwilling and resistant to ideas to help the child thrive in their classrooms? While I wonder about these teachers, I also have questions about systems that demand perfect conditions in the classrooms for the sake of compliance with onerous, ever changing learning standards. Systems that demand and yet do not provide the support that teachers need to do their work, either in terms of compensation or having more humans employed to assist them. I have questions too for a system like the ones in the state I live in, those that give the tenure that affords teachers life-long jobs in schools and districts that are getting more diverse by the day, but the teachers are white as can be. These districts with teachers who do not see the need to raise their cultural awareness to ensure that kids in their classrooms get those equal opportunities that the educational system promises every child.

THE BELONGING PARADOX

Reflecting back to my son growing up. The exclusion was done by the adults. The children would play together at school, and get along quite well. Then somehow we would learn that someone had a birthday party and he was not invited or involved. We never really spoke about it, but I noticed it. I always had activities for my son to participate in, so I was not reliant on him and I being invited somewhere in order to have something to do. Through these activities, he developed many skills and friendships that he has kept over the years. While I would never deliberately leave out a child, I think it is unfortunate that the insecurity of individuals keeps their lives closed and within a bubble.

What would I tell my child now?

I would teach my child to know that kindness must be the default at all times. That people and places that are not kind to others will eventually not be kind to him/her. That kindness means sometimes doing or being what the group is not doing or being. I would teach him how to stand up for himself if he was being criticized or ostracized for wanting to be inclusive of those considered as outcasts. I would also make sure that my child's world is expansive and filled with creativity and adventure.

~ SA

Of Neuro-Diverse Children (and Parent)

Why did I decide eventually to talk about the journey of parenting as a working mother in a book on belonging? Because every time my child came home with a report or every time I got a call from the psychologist, it felt like I had been placed before judge and jury and found wanting (and guilty). Many of the emotions, chiefly the shame I thought I had outgrown as the child who never seemed to get it together (except when reading books and daydreaming), came flooding back. This was no longer simply about my parenting, but about me. Because I saw myself reflected in my children.

Although I can be considered a pretty successful adult, I have always known that part of my ability to make it (at work and life) was the result of the boundaries and routines learned in my Nigerian boarding school. Not that I did not have comments about organization and talking too much on my term report cards, but somehow I made it through the six years spent there. But, throughout my life, I have always suffered from catastrophic thinking from a brain (and mired) wired the way mine was. I remember always being deathly afraid of forgetting important dates or appointments, or other such things that would mark me for life due to their career-ending nature. Now you might be thinking, "Who walks around with these kinds of thoughts?" It does not change the fact that I carried these fears around like a weighted ankle ball and chain. I did my best to work within the boundaries that life had offered and I made sure (I thought), to choose a profession and roles that fit my proclivities. I knew there were areas where

THE BELONGING PARADOX

I was expected to show up a certain way and I managed to make it work through what I have come to know as "masking."[1]

With the subsequent arrival of my sons into this carefully curated life, I began to see certain traits of boundless expressiveness and creativity and brilliance. I made sure to nourish their budding minds and their creativity as best as I could while enjoying being a mother to them. That is until my Child 2 went to school and there was no room for him and his type of neurodivergence.

His non-belonging at school was mine, it felt to me. The teachers complaining about him could as well have been complaining about me. The massive criticism wore on him, and led to a huge dislike of school. I debated about homeschooling but knew it would be a (surmountable?) challenge due to my own ways of being. I knew he needed structure, the way I had gotten it, but how were we to do it with his unique personality? I remember so many nights asking God if there was any other way to make the process of my sons living their own neurodivergent lives easier, and to please show me on their behalf. All I knew was to bolster their self-esteem and confidence at home with mommy love, affection, and attention. Although my semi-flexible work schedule meant I could be present physically for school related activities, I needed ways to be more emotionally present for them (and for myself too).

The Nurture Debts We Owe and Are Owed

As a child raised in Africa, the implicit expectation on us was that we were being raised for communal gains. With the external influence from extensive globalization and observing other cultural thought patterns, some have started to buck these expectations. In spite of this, the obligations persist.

Now that I have my own children, I do not imagine yet that they owe me anything, because they are still so young. On the contrary, I owe my children a lot of gratitude for my apparent emancipation. I tell anyone who cares to listen that my children came into my life to save me from myself. This book and all the research and questions that went into writing it would not exist but for the unique personalities of the children I am privileged to parent. Life with them has been a personal anthropological study. Because of them, I finally got the courage to reflect on who I was, who I am, and who I want to be as a person, and as a mother. Seeing them face many of the challenges I faced as a child allowed me to sit back and ask if it was an accident of time and place or if it was mostly nature. The answers I found and I am finding have helped me come home to myself and hopefully will help me build a home for them where they can thrive and blossom in a world that they belong in.

⋆⋆⋆⋆⋆

THE BELONGING PARADOX

One of the things I did was to research everything about ADHD and being twice exceptional (the name for gifted children) and find books and practitioners who reinforce a positive outlook. Research and advocate. Rinse and repeat.

If there is anything I know for sure, it is that I will continue to carry the torch of advocacy for my sons until I am physically unable to. In researching and teaching them how to be themselves, I found that I was also teaching myself. Every day of accepting, acknowledging, and coming to terms with what lay ahead if I was going to help the boys create their path for success found me accepting myself too. In reminding them that ADHD did not mean there was something wrong or off kilter, I remind myself as well as we jointly walk this path. Parenting helped me find myself as a human with gifts to offer the world I inhabit, starting with my family.

Whether or not you are a parent of a child or children with special needs, trying to be all things to your children while trying to live your life and build a career is not easy. I acknowledge you and the work it takes. For those who have decided to make their children their career, I honor you and the sacrifices you are making. Whichever way you and I choose, we must think in terms of community and solidarity and regeneration. We were not meant to parent alone, as humans in a social system. Do not buy into the lies that make it seem like your child's upbringing and how they turn out is your sole responsibility. Find community. Share community. If we can bring back our parental belonging, from a place of self-awareness and humility, our children and us will be the better for it. I know, because I have walked this path. I learned to cast off the shame around any uninformed judgments of my children, and therefore of my parenting. I remind myself that to have made it this far is by the grace of God. I remind parents around me who choose to hear that we are not meant to journey alone. I am your biggest advocate on this journey. Being a parent and aunty to children on the spectrum, I have had a front row seat to the power of love and advocacy and family bonds in ensuring parental belonging. And I want the same for you too.

THE BELONGING PARADOX

Friendships and Parental Belonging: Different Worldviews

While I spent the most of this chapter on belonging as a parent(s) of a neurodivergent child, another area where one can experience fluctuating belonging in parenting is seen with differences in parenting-life stages between parent-friends. If you are a person who married later (or earlier) than your friends, and these friends started their parenting journeys much earlier, it stands to reason that their worldviews and loyalties will necessarily shift as their lives become focused on this new phase of their lives.

It takes intentional effort to maintain your relationships in certain stages of parenting. If you become a new parent but have friends with children who are heading to college, you may find that you no longer have much in (parenting) common. In my case, I was and still am fortunate to have mom-physician friends, one of whom is a stellar emergency care pediatrician. Although her children were much older than mine by far, at every point during my children's toddler years, I had her as a physician advocate and friend. I knew she was only a phone call away. I also knew as a result of our being tightly knit friends that her love for my children was boundless even as she served as a reservoir of wisdom and discipline and care. I had someone to talk to about issues, to enter into my story regarding my children and their diagnosis.

◆◆◆◆◆

Having many friends on speed dial to answer my numerous parenting questions or for recommendations whenever my children were sick had such a significant impact on my parenting life and belonging state. I am grateful for the many parent-friends in my life in the country we all now call home. I am sure that if you too look around and within your degrees of friendship circles, you will find friends who are happy and willing to help you lighten your parenting load, no matter where in the world you are.

THE BELONGING PARADOX

A Researcher-Parent and Educator's Notes

For readers asking about findings from my research on parenting techniques, I list some resources here. I admittedly gravitated toward books that did not take a pathological approach to diagnosis and treatment but rather reframed ADHD (and its co-location with giftedness) in more positive terms. These are some of the many that I found applicable to our family situation.

- **The Organized Child** (*Richard Gallagher, Elana G. Spira and Jennifer L. Rosenblatt*)
- **The Smart But Scattered Guide to Success** *(Peg Dawson and Richard Guare)*
- **Smart But Scattered Teens** *(Richard Guare, Peg Dawson, and Colin Guare)*
- **Answers to Distraction** *(Edward M. Hallowell, MD and John J. Ratey, MD)*
- **Gifted and Distractible** *(Julie F. Skolnick)*
- **Embracing the Whole Gifted Self** *(Patricia Gatto-Walden PhD)*
- **Journey into Your Rainforest Mind** *(Paula Prober)*

And of course, **ADDItude**, the wildly popular ADD blog and magazine.*

I am aware that many parents of neurodivergent and gifted children have done their own research (resourcefulness is a

---

*https://www.additudemag.com/

watchword for parents like me). I am also aware that many have their own referent frames about what works for them and their children. Therefore, in listing any resources here, I make no endorsements or claims to their effectiveness.

School Choices: Conflict Resolution

From a resource perspective, I must not fail to reflect on what we must do as parents to ensure that our children are not relegated to the problem corner in spaces meant to make room for them (such as schools).

We must be ready to act on our child's behalf to let them see and know that they belong. As a parent, I consider it my responsibility to be an advocate voice for my child, in ways that I wish my own parents had done for me. In saying this, I am in no way advocating for a child-centered world or one where children can do no wrong. I am that parent who will work with my children's teachers to enforce necessary discipline because I want them to grow up into kind, responsible humans who are mindful of others.

From my family's experience though, I have seen that advocacy from a woman like me always comes at a cost. But it is a price I am willing to pay to ensure that my children belong at school much as they do at home.

Advocating for our children can sometimes feel like walking into a conflict situation. Which it is, since conflict typically arises from two opposing points of view. With ADHD in our case, it might be differences in opinion between using medication for the child versus trying out behavior therapy and other accommodations. It would be harmful to our sense of wellbeing then to come into any school related conversations and meetings with a win-lose mentality. A win-

THE BELONGING PARADOX

win mindset is needed in many instances because most parents and teachers want the same outcomes: a well-adjusted child, able to learn without issues. With that in mind, we can approach potentially conflictual situations in three stages:

1) **Pre-Meeting**: At this stage, the work is on emotional regulation and setting goals. Think about how you want to feel during and after the meeting. Think about the potential for the meeting to take different turns and what you might do if this happens. Decide too, on the outcome you want to have from the meeting.
2) **During the Meeting**: Here, focus on reflective listening and taking notes, Listen without interruption. When it is your turn, ask to speak without being interrupted. Rebut any points raised that you feel strongly about. Do this without an accusatory tone. At the end, ask for help with setting common goals for all parties and clarify stated goals.
3) **After the meeting:** Send thank you emails and reiterate the common goals agreed on at the meeting and let all know a time frame to check back on progress.

Many of these steps are strategies developed over time that I use in school meetings about my children. The emotional regulation pre-meeting practice is useful as it helps me draw boundaries before any interactions so that my belonging state as a parent is not impacted unduly (see The BELONG framework). I have shared these techniques with many parents wanting similar outcomes for their children, and I am now including them here as one part of community-centered work to enhance belonging for parents like me.

Belonging Corner Reflections

1) Do you tie your belonging as a parent to that of your child being accepted in certain spaces? How can you separate the two things while helping your child overcome feelings of non-belonging?
2) As you reflect on spaces in your parenting life, how do you think you can offer others a sense of acceptance and belonging? Are you giving acceptance to those around you?
3) If you are a parent to children with special needs, what spaces have been the most welcoming and accepting of you and your children that helped shore up your sense of belonging?
4) In this book, I have talked about giving signals of belonging to others around us. What are some signals of belonging that you would have loved to have as a parent of a differently abled child? How can you create and reflect those signals outward to other parents and children alike?

PART VI

Belonging: A Brief Explainer, or Two

A person is a person through other persons. None of us comes into the world fully formed…We need other human beings in order to be human.

— Archbishop Desmond Tutu

Belonging: A Brief Explainer, or Two

As we evolve, so also should the questions we ask of ourselves. But some questions need not evolve, in particular, questions related to belonging.

What is Belonging?

When all is said and done, this simple question still begs for answers. In response, I want to begin with a perspective from two cultural worldviews.

For people in more sociocentric societies (as found in many African communities), belonging and the need to belong was not differentiated from other physical (or psychological) needs. In these societies, one's belonging was assured by virtue of birth. It was from such a sociocultural worldview that French Congolese Philosopher Jean Masamba Ma Mpolo—in opposition to Rene Descartes's *"cogito ergo sum" (in English, "I think therefore I am")*—wrote:

> *"Traditional cultures define the individual's identity in the following ontological formula: "Cognatus ergo sum" [or] "I belong, therefore I am." To belong is to participate and contribute to the welfare of the family. This is in opposition to the individualistic dictum of Descartes…It is not the individual's capacity to think which is the prime source of his or her identity formation, but rather the reality and the ability of belonging, participating and sharing…."*[1]

If you have ever heard of the Ubuntu philosophy, you would recognize its underpinnings in Ma Mpolo's words.[2] I am an African by ancestry and birth and so I understand this relational form of personhood where you are seen as a person through communal relationship. Here, a person's belonging came by virtue of birth into their extended family within a community.

"Humans are social creatures", we have heard ad nauseum. If so, how did Western civilizations reach what I call a nadir of selfhood by insisting that we can exist without others, when our personhood can only be fully seen and reflected in the presence of others. This communal reflection of personhood, to me, is what belonging is all about. It is within this context that I now return to the various definitions of belonging out there, definitions that have in some form or shape permeated my thinking, and my writing.

∗∗∗∗∗

The most referenced and cited work on belonging in the United States is from the extensive review done by Roy Baumeister and Mark Leary in 1995 in a publication titled *"The Need to Belong: Desire for Interpersonal Attachments as a Fundamental Human Motivation"*[3] (yes, we academics were actually taught to write like this). According to Baumeister and Leary, belonging is good and the need to belong is a deeply rooted human need that feeds into how we think, feel, and behave. They highlight key features that help humans satisfy belonging needs, including:

i) Frequent, relatively positive, and conflict-free personal contacts or interactions with people that we are in relationship with.
ii) A belief that these interpersonal interactions have some sense of stability and longevity, and are marked with concern for our welfare.

> iii) The belief that these relationships and interactions are based on mutual trust and reciprocity.*

Findings from their work include the fact that the need for belonging (although good and desired), can be fulfilled in ways that threaten people's health and that of others in a functioning society. People for example, who find their sense of belonging through membership in groups that dehumanize others and consider them unworthy of respect or affection, may be fulfilling belonging needs but are doing so in fundamentally unhealthy ways.

They also categorically showed that many of the negative emotions we have from experiences of non-belonging lessen over time as we grow. Feelings of rejection from not belonging are most experienced in adolescence and young adulthood, based on an overvaluing of acceptance from others. As we get older, we become more discerning about where acceptance and belonging matters (or not). This is why some people can stay on at jobs in unfriendly or unhealthy environments. Because they have learned to place more value on earning money (and being a provider for their families) versus being the golden boy or girl at work.

One more finding from their work that I find relevant to my thinking is that of valuations of relationships with respect to belonging. They state, as I have come to appreciate in real life when speaking of other's acceptance of us, that we cannot like everyone, and everyone cannot like us. The human brain

---

* These are also relational qualities ascribed to communal personhood within the Ubuntu philosophy. The idea that your people love you, are there for you and will always be your people, to whom you belong.

does not have the capacity to hold everyone in our social circles at the same level of affiliation and affection. Understanding this should not be a problem. The problem according to them is that as humans, we let our implicit reactions to people be affected; by traits and characteristics that have nothing to do with their actual relational value; characteristics like skin color, gender, and nationality. As a result, we tend to turn our backs on people we may very well be better off knowing. Following which, we (inadvertently) turn around and disadvantage them in small and big ways.

This is a problem that looms large in pluralistic and tribalistic societies, of which America is one example. So, the question to ask instead should be "How can we value people for who they are without making unproven judgments on their social acceptability based on perceived characteristics and traits?" This is the quintessential question we must answer if we are to make room for increased belonging for the people around us (no matter who, what, or where they are).

Other Definitions and Conceptions of Belonging:

Belonging is the general inference we draw from cues, events, experiences and relationships about our potential for fit or of the quality of fit between us and others in social settings. Belonging is experienced and includes the feeling of being accepted, included, respected in, and contributing to such settings.[4]

~ Gregory M. Walton and Shannon T. Brady

An important takeaway from this definition is that no two persons will draw the same inferences about the quality of their belonging experience in any particular space. In making these inferences, people ask questions like, "Do I have anything in common with the people in this place?" "Are people like me valued and listened to in this environment?" Asking these kinds of questions can lead individuals to respond to cues that appear minor (or even invisible) to other people who are not asking these types of internal questions. My goal is not to write a thesis on belonging definitions since there are as many definitions out there as there are theories. I will instead focus on dimensions of belonging from the perspective of faith and community (one of life areas covered in this book).

⋆⋆⋆⋆⋆

In *Three Pieces of Glass*, author Eric Jacobsen paraphrased Joseph Myers's work and defined belonging *as a nuanced, complex and coherent phenomenon, one essential for human flourishing*.[5] He wrote that human belonging included geographical, social and cultural dimensions, as I also describe in The BELONG framework. Jacobsen reflects too on different levels of experiential belonging in different spaces and contexts, based off the work of Edward T. Hall, the late American sociologist. He describes distinct levels of belonging—intimate, personal, social and public—governed by different rules for spatial relations. Jacobsen writes that these four levels through providing context for relational experiences within them, both communicate, and reinforce belonging.

The four dimensions are:

a) *Intimate belonging* as seen with a spouse or perhaps a best friend. We do not keep secrets from those with whom we experience intimate belonging.
b) *Personal belonging* is experienced with our families and close friends. We are very close to people with whom we experience personal belonging.
c) *Social belonging* is what we experience with people we recognize but may not yet know very well. We experience social belonging at church, or at a PTA meeting. Social belonging is important for boosting identity formation, and there is a tendency to both overlook and underestimate its role in our lives. In settings that enable social belonging, we have to explain who we are to other people and often, it is in providing answers that we figure out who we are and what we stand for. Social belonging also feeds into personal and intimate belonging because it is from many social settings that we often self-select those with whom we experience personal or intimate belonging.
d) *Public belonging* is seen with people we may not know personally but we are nevertheless connected through certain common threads. Public belonging is what we experience with other fans of a sports team, or with other residents in the same town.[6]

These definitions of belonging dimensions speak to one of the conclusions from Baumeister and Leary's work. The ideas that as adults, belonging is not a pressing need in many spaces. They give a familiar example; that of a person joining an association. A person might join such an association only because a job requires it from them. They do not join with a goal of fulfilling belonging needs. In fact, some who join these associations may not actually care much for groups or for the networking demands of these spaces. They do it only because they have to. Therefore, being accepted (or not) makes no difference in the grand scheme of their life since their reason for joining was to fulfill a mandatory job-related function. On the other hand, people crave and desire belonging in those spaces they consider meaningful in their lives. It is therefore in these meaningful life spaces that one must do the work of belonging and learning to belong.

THE BELONGING PARADOX

PART VII

A Walk Through the Paradox of Belonging

The experience of darkness has been essential to my coming into selfhood, and telling the truth about that fact helps me stay in the light. But I want to tell the truth for another reason as well... many young people today journey in the dark as the young always have, and we elders do them a disservice when we withhold the shadowy parts of our lives. When I was young, there were very few elders willing to talk about the darkness; most of them pretended that success was all they had ever known. As the darkness began to descend upon me in my early twenties, I thought I had developed a unique and terminal case of failure. I did not realize I had merely embarked on a journey toward joining the human race.

—Parker J Palmer[1]

THE BELONGING PARADOX

I wrote this book to explore a different kind of darkness within. To shine a light on what I knew to be a paradox of belonging. Actually, two paradoxes.

1: Belonging is an Internal (Trait) and External Process (State).

Anywhere there is a group of people, there will be belonging pressures. I currently live in the US, and have told stories both of belonging and non-belonging that happened either to me or to those who shared their stories here with me. Growing up, in my birth country, I also experienced non-belonging at different developmental stages. Which is to say that there will be different external geographic markers that may serve to situate one's belonging in place (or place-belonging).

For instance, with external geographic place-belonging, the conferment of United States citizenship on me was one I had to work for by following immigration guidelines and procedures. Once the process was complete, I received the same rights as those born here (except for nominations for the office of president, and other top security clearance positions). All the belonging rights of citizens are mine, unless I break the terms of agreement, then the citizenship contract is deemed revocable. Knowing this allows me to carry on and to live my life here uninterrupted, no matter what those born here may try to tell me.

In this case of national belonging, I must recognize that sometimes what I may see and experience is a response to what people born in America perceive as a shift in the national internal family system. A shift in family systems (as seen with the birth or adoption of a child into an existing family) can evoke corresponding responses that is not the fault of the newcomer. Internal family systems can have a huge impact on our state belonging and sometimes much of our lives is spent trying to regain any equilibrium we believe is missing. Hence the continual search for belonging from people outside. But we cannot demand of others what is already ours. We were born to belong. No one can give us belonging. We have to give it to ourselves. Belonging traverses both states and borders.

> "I belong simply because I am."

2: We Can Be Ourselves Within and Without Community.

The search for belonging includes wading through the ever-present tension between wanting to be yourself and wanting to be an integral part of others in group settings. To truly belong, one must work on the life concept of being an individual-in-community. By individual, I do not mean individualism as practiced in Western cultures. Individualism as a way of life has been tried and found wanting due to its unspoken but embodied practices of attempting to place the individual above communal bonds, through both functional and transactional commitments.[2] For us to encounter true belonging, we need to practice and make ways for others to be themselves while still being grounded in community.

THE BELONGING PARADOX

To be an individual then, in the sense I write of here, is to be an indivisible whole, to exist in congruence with oneself, and to have marked individuality. Our individuality consists of those traits and behaviors that are unique to us and help distinguish us from others of our kind (or other humans). Individuality is the process of differentiation, how we develop differences in connection with others, how we learn to be contextually versatile and adaptable.[2] This is similar to biological differentiation; a process where immature cells in the body differentiate into organs while still being a part of the central system.[3]

Differentiation produces organs with unique roles that serve to ensure that the body works as designed. So also, when we are differentiated as individuals-in-community, we are free to serve the body (or group) well, and through the group, we ourselves are served. The differentiation I speak of affords individuals the freedom to adapt and match their behaviors to different social situations, a skill I consider similar to cultural intelligence.[4] With cultural intelligence, we learn to be adaptively different in different social contexts without changing the essence of who we are. When we learn how to be truly individual, we will have no issues being in community with people who are different from us.

ions.

The HOW TO Section

A FRAMEWORK FOR LIVED BELONGING

Talk about belonging is not relegated as some trivial aspect of our lives. I mentioned the Baumeister and Leary paper on belonging. This work has been cited over 35,000 times, which for those in the business of research publication, speaks about the reach of this seminal work that established belonging as a fundamental human motivation. With this book, I built on those findings in a unique way. I am clear on one thing, that others who have not lived our lives, should not be the ones telling us how to belong, especially for those of us who have learned to exist in liminal spaces over time.

The BELONG framework presented here gets its foundation from my work on belonging and my lived experience in cross-cultural environments. I consider it a framework for living belonging; a navigator's guide to enhancing belonging in different life spaces. Use as needed for your belonging journey. For anyone who works with people who are different from you (which happens to be all the time), use this framework to see life through their lens. Then turn to the next sections for recommended practices to help foster belonging for yourself and others.

A Framework for Lived Belonging

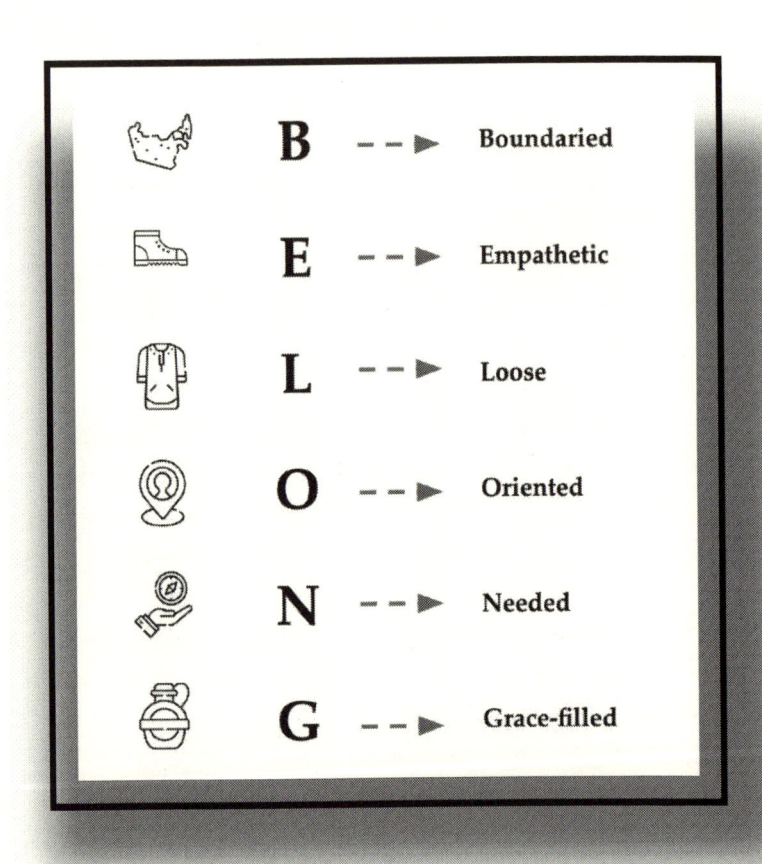

	B	--▶	Boundaried
	E	--▶	Empathetic
	L	--▶	Loose
	O	--▶	Oriented
	N	--▶	Needed
	G	--▶	Grace-filled

The BELONG framework

THE BELONGING PARADOX

☐ BOUNDARIED

True belonging needs boundaries. Although it appears I have made a case in this book for belonging no matter who or what, we cannot belong everywhere. We should not seek to belong everywhere without reason. Knowing where to expend finite energy is a skill. Learning how to belong to oneself provides the gateway to building up many of the skills required for the initial step in The BELONG framework.

For example, as a relatively risk averse and conservative person, you would not find me spending my time or energy trying to belong to a group of bikers (no offense to all the sleek Harley Davidson bike riders). I cannot go to this group and depend on them to satisfy my belonging needs, because I do not share any intrinsic or extrinsic affiliation with them. This is not to say that if I did go, members of the group would not accept me. To say otherwise, would be to project about the behaviors of members of the group.

In this step, the responsibility lies with us as differentiated individuals, to recognize and know our belonging boundaries; where to be, where to go, what we need, and what we have to give or offer others. To be attuned to belonging boundary lines provides the ability to draw and redraw them as necessary. This allows us make adequate room for people who want to share space with us and for the people we want to share spaces with. When we practice offering more fully of ourselves, it invites others to belong as well.

▢ EMPATHETIC

To be empathetic is to have the skill of being able to walk a mile in another's shoes. The empathy adopted in this framework is an enriching bidirectional kind. Radical empathy—an internally and externally oriented empathy—is a skill that can be learned. We practice radical empathy through an intentional choice to enter into the consciousness of others' experiences.[1,2] In doing so, we find ourselves enriched by the similarities between any parts of our experience and that of people in relationship with us, while respecting the differences in our experiences. To be empathetic is to respect the distinctness of self, both in oneself and in others. It is also to seek to enhance other people's individual boundaries as they walk through the process of sharing any parts of their lives with us.

With radical empathy, we empathize with the parts of ourselves that have been impacted by instances and experiences of rejection or non-inclusion. We also get to direct that empathy outward to others around us. If you have experienced non-belonging and how it made you feel, you now know what it takes to prevent others from being excluded, be it from certain spaces or from opportunities.

▢ LOOSE

Be loose. A type of loose I refer to as 'shake-loose' — shake loose from attachment to outcomes. If we go into spaces expecting a certain fixed outcome and meet disappointment, it

THE BELONGING PARADOX

could lead to feelings of hurt (and rejection). Because the stories we tell and the meanings we make from interpersonal experiences can impact our state belonging, we need to hold belonging stories loosely and be ready to reframe them as quickly as they were created (See Mora's story in section 1). The practice of being loose counteracts the impact of other people's actions on our sense of belonging. Shaking loose enables a quick shift in belonging states, much like wet dogs shake water off their fur to change their state as they move from wet to dry environments, all the while maintaining their core self. If we learn how to shift our state belonging (from low to high) in the aftermath of unfulfilling belonging experiences, it helps us enhance core belonging. This is similar to learning to change certain aspects of our personality with time, despite how stable our core personality might be.

ORIENTED

To be oriented is to locate ourselves in our environment with respect to time, place and people. It involves knowing how and where we stand and most importantly what we stand for. As a former international student, now employee and citizen, orientation brings back memories of locations and re-locations. Here, I think of events like international student orientation or new hire orientation that were meant to situate me properly into my new environment at the time. I cannot speak of orientation with respect to belonging without talking about culture and values, as this is an area that people like me who identify as first (or second) generation immigrants struggle with. As an immigrant, orientation in The BELONG framework makes room for a unique duality in social identification—learning the customs and practices of new spaces and places, while keeping and honoring one's ancestral roots. A healthy ability to identify with new social environments can help foster belonging. Orienting ourselves well enables the type of adaptation where we get to choose to keep the core parts of our culture while absorbing new ones. A process known as acculturation as opposed to cultural assimilation where people essentially lose themselves in the new culture.[3] Orientation is essential for self-knowledge and values identification, so that in whatever time, place, or space we find ourselves, we are able to locate our own people, those who will welcome us and situate us among them. Once oriented, we can help others in our environments get situated, and in this way enhance belonging for them.

☐ NEEDED

We cannot fully belong if we do not recognize the fact that we are needed. We are needed simply based on our existence at this time in the spaces we are in. This needfulness must not be confused with neediness, something that society has somehow convinced us is bad, in that to be needy is synonymous with co-dependency or loneliness. This part of the framework charges us to recognize that we are filling a need in the spaces we find ourselves. As children, we meet the need for addition to families as someone's child. On an adult note, we are needed at work, even with at-will employment and its emphasis on the transience and disposability of labor.

We are needed as we make our way through life. Needed to become the future persons that we are currently in the process of becoming. And for that to happen—much like a butterfly in the process of becoming what it was born to be, needs time to pass from larvae to pupa to full blown beauty—we need time, and space. To enter into the fullness of belonging, we need the time to weather multiple belonging experiences, and to know that the world needs us in our present self. We need space to accept ourselves (and others) as we continue to find our place in the world.

☐ GRACE-FILLED

If boundaries are what we used to constrain the beginning, grace is the open-ended cap of The BELONG framework. Grace, in this living framework is not to be confused with the short prayer we learned to say before meals, but rather a two-dimensional construct:

1. As spiritual concept— grace is a profound unearned gift that one did nothing to deserve. Belonging is something we must grace ourselves and others with. As humans, it can be hard to turn away from status and country-club mindsets, but true belonging should not come with conditions. Which is why this aspect of the framework transcends what we can do in our human capacity. Grace is not transactional. It does not seek for or need *quid pro quos*. Grace is gifted, even without asking. When we are grace-filled, we can grace others with belonging. We are able to help others belong because we have given ourselves the gift of belonging.
2. As quality or state— to be grace-filled is to be thoughtful and considerate. When we apply grace in belonging, we are

thoughtful and considerate of ourselves and of others. We acknowledge our strengths and shortcomings and accept them with equanimity. We do not think too highly or too lowly of ourselves and others. This balancing act allows us to maintain perspective, which allows for positive reinterpretations of the many inevitable situations where belonging uncertainty may abound. And to do so with grace. This extension of grace toward ambiguous events and experiences, can mimic cognitive behavioral techniques, all of which we can use to close belonging gaps.

THE BELONGING PARADOX

Bringing Belonging Back to Yourself (and Others)

We must by necessity and love for our fellow humans, create spaces where signals of belonging are rampant and clear for all, no matter who they are.

Why, you ask?

Because inferences about belonging do not stay only in our heads. When we experience negative or positive belonging signals, we make inferences about these experiences in the present. These inferences tend to become self-fulfilling due to confirmation bias as we unconsciously look for cues to support our conclusions and our state belonging. Therefore, when we help others positively reinforce their sense of belonging, we help ourselves too as we develop relationship capital in different settings. In our attempts to build belonging for others, we need to ensure belonging cues and signals (smiles, introductions to other group members, collective lunches) are delivered early on in our interpersonal interactions as this is when they tend to be the most beneficial.

So, how do we go about bringing belonging to ourselves and others?

To Enhance Belonging, Don't Just Sit or Stand. Do Something

The environment we are in can be a determinant of our state belonging. To use an analogy from basic plant genetics; a seed is germinated with complete genetic potential but the environment where it is planted determines how well it grows. Growth stunts can happen when seeds are not in the right environment. The same with belonging. Being in the wrong environment can cripple belonging as it may take longer to realize potential because of external signals that make us think there is something wrong with us as persons. The flip side to this environmental relationship is that the same environment with the potential to cripple belonging can also accelerate the decision to replant and find nourishment elsewhere. Taking a human view to my seed analogy, while seeds cannot uproot and replant themselves, the same cannot be said of human beings. The very human ability to strategize, flex, and adapt can lead to a purposeful uprooting and replanting in a healthier environment. The downside is that some have never experienced stable and nourishing environments to use for comparisons in a bid to build or restore belonging through relocations. It is for people like this that I do this work. This book would not be complete therefore without presenting ways to keep calm, and learn to belong. This is the **'How To'** part of the Paradox — how to enable and practice true belonging for yourself and others.

> "We belong even when we do not think or feel like we belong"

Ways to Practice Belonging

I began this book by showcasing individual belonging and non-belonging stories that framed a sense of belonging in binary terms, one either belonged or not. To facilitate true belonging, I now make the case for active movement—away from binaries and into a paradox mindset.

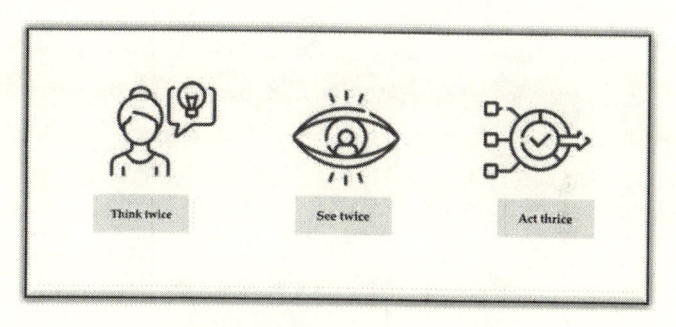

The Belonging Practices: Sensory Modes

In the next couple of pages, I will focus on practical thinking modes, behaviors, and shifts that enable this movement. What I also refer to as 'Sensory Modes' of belonging practices; how we can see and think differently, and then act to enhance belonging (You can skip to the end for the TL;DR or too long; didn't read version of these practices).

First: HOW TO THINK

We are not limited or condemned to binary [black or white] thinking
—Wiliam R. Miller

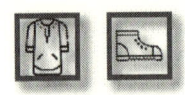

1. Think in Opposites (or Think Dialectically)

Developing the ability to view belonging from multiple perspectives is a necessary skill for relationships and attendant belonging experiences. With dialectical thinking, we recognize that two conflicting things can be true at the same time.[1]

Going back to the concept of evocation introduced in the belonging at work section, the practice of dialectic thinking can be applied as follows:

Non-belonging
E → → → → → P

*The environment (E) may respond to my presence by sending signals of non-belonging through other people's behaviors, **yet** as a person, (P) I belong because I am (here).*

THE BELONGING PARADOX

With dialectical thinking, person (P) can acknowledge the unwelcoming environment and also recognize that non-belonging signals from the environment were not initiated by them. Learning about evocation helped me apply dialectic thinking regarding my work experiences. I recognized my supervisor's unwelcoming behavior alongside the knowledge that all the apparently discriminatory behavior was not from anything I did wrong.

Dialectical thinking with its ability to hold two opposing things (views) can help break the false dichotomy that many of us have been led to believe about ourselves as persons, P. This dichotomy, based on the false conclusion that not belonging or fitting in is our fault alone and has nothing to do with the environment.

2. Think About Your Agency

Do not feel lonely, the entire universe is inside you.
—Rumi

As human beings, we have what psychologists call agency. This agency is seen in Carl Rogers's definition of a whole and fully functioning individual as one who:

- takes responsibility for their actions (and consequences) based on a recognition of their freedom and power to choose from the many options that life makes available.
- can creatively adjust to changing conditions as they arise.[2]

Such a person can relate to society without feeling overly bound by traditions, conventions, or societal norms; they can act on their own behalf.

This wholesome conception of self enables us create spaces of belonging for ourselves and by design, for others. In-depth self-acceptance helps us make sense of the behaviors and acceptance (or not) of others. This knowing also provides what we need to act on our own behalf as agentic beings, similar to what Mora did for her family in her story regarding the perceived rejection from her homeschooling community. When we accept ourselves, we can accept others and they in turn are free to accept us. As a result of radical self-acceptance, we can, when people do not fully accept us, decide to limit interactions with them (a form of boundary setting). Remember, "*You have to belong to yourself before you can belong to others.*"

Next: HOW TO SEE

To exist is to be perceived
—Bishop George Berkeley

1. See Belonging Through an Existential Lens

Existential therapists believe that people's existence can be charted across four dimensions: physical, social, psychological and spiritual.[3] Our encounters with the world shape our attitudes based on our framing of our experiences. In other words, our orientation toward the world can define our reality. A process that is best summed by the saying "We see the world as we are."

While belonging can track with physical time and space— for example as a woman born in Africa (Nigeria), now living in America, these two places leave me with different degrees of belonging— the focus of this book is mostly on social belonging. On the social dimension, we interact with the world surrounding us on the basis of either the culture we were brought up in, the culture we live in, or the class and race we were born into. Our attitudes and responses based on these interactions can range from cooperation to competition or from love to hate. Much the same way, we can teeter between belonging and non-belonging. I for one still see humans as fully capable of kindness, in spite of people who might behave contrary to this perception (in the light of stories in this book).

From an existential standpoint then, how do we keep the pendulum swinging more toward belonging?

We do this by recognizing and accepting the duality of being a human in relationship with others, the duality of acceptance and rejection. We must see that being accepted or rejected in one space does not translate as reality in every other space. In terms of rejection, it may be that the space was not the right one for us at that moment or season, regardless of how much we want to belong (or fit in).

For true belonging, we acknowledge and accept our human wants and desires around belonging and what I call the 'go-no-go' motivations that accompany these desires. When we recognize that wanting to belong in certain places and spaces is part of the human experience, we can stop asking ourselves the wrong questions. Questions like "What is wrong with me?" "Why don't people like me?" "What can I do to fit in?" These types of questions are unhelpful because they take a person-first view of the problem instead of considering heterogeneity of person-environment interactions in different life spaces.

Accepting the duality underlying belonging needs and experiences keeps us from being stuck. When we are unstuck, we are free to use our agency. Free to create spaces of belonging within and without. As a free agent, some decisions we take regarding environments where we experience non-belonging may involve leaving the environment. It may mean staying and learning to find sources of meaningful experiences, independent of people's validation of us, as difficult as this might be.

2. See a Reflected Sense of Belonging

> *We must be our own before we can be another's.*
> —Ralph Waldo Emerson

We cannot separate our life from our experiences. Which is why the feeling of belonging or non-belonging can be so personal. Who am I if others do not accept me for who I am and for the ways in which I conceive myself? Building belonging involves learning to function from a healthy sense of self in order to bring the 'be' back in belonging. With this practice, we recognize that our experiences can sometimes shift our sense of belonging, but we can organize and reorganize those experiences in creative and effective ways to help us maintain a positive outlook.

By organization of experiences, I do not mean a "file and forget" ideology where well-meaning coaches and motivational speakers tell us to think through our thoughts. There is nothing wrong with these techniques, I use them all the time. With this practice, I go a step further and remind us to see ourselves as we are, thinking and feeling creatures who decipher through physical and emotional sensation.

With reorganization of belonging experiences, we refuse to take in the messages and signals of non-belonging that people try to project toward us. Here, we can also respond flexibly by participating in any activities designed to foster belonging knowing that our identities do not have to be completely submerged. Through reorganization, we learn to deconstruct fixed identities of ourselves as persons who do or do not belong. We recognize that many identities we foist on ourselves are not fixed but rather are (temporary) descriptions based on our experiences. If we see these descriptions as the temporary identities that they are, we can, with sufficient support, learn to discard them.[4]

Undoing previously fixed identities is not going to be automatic. We will have to walk through new spaces which in themselves may evoke feelings of discomfort, anxiety, or shame. To experience full belonging, we will have to work through the very uncomfortable and sometimes shameful feelings of non-belonging. This is normal. But in creating or finding new spaces, little by little we will begin to see that there is room for everyone, even for people who feel like they do not belong.

The paradoxical nature of this particular practice is that as humans, we can reflect belonging to others because we already belong, not because we are trying to belong or fit in. We begin the process of reflected belonging by accepting who we are. Then as we find spaces where our full persons are accepted, the world opens up, we open up, and we become signal beacons of belonging for others.

THE BELONGING PARADOX

Then: HOW TO ACT

Whatever you wish that others would do to you, do also to them...
—The Book of Matthew Chapter 7 verse 12 (ESV)

1. Strengthen Your Core. Clarify Core Values

Understanding our core values and beliefs is crucial for shaping identity and belonging. Human values are both **objective** and **subjective**. Objective values like love, justice and harmony ensure a working society. Subjective values are as the name suggests, subjective. No two humans will have the exact list of preferred values. As "To thine own self be true" in Shakespeare's Hamlet, so it is with core values. Our core values are those we consider true to our own self, our self-concept, and identity.[5]

Speaking then in this language of values, belonging is a two-sided value because it can be placed as objective and subjective. As an objective value, most people generally agree that belonging is of value for a fairer society. For certain others like me, belonging is not just a nice to have, it is a core value.

Placing Belonging as a Value

As individuals in social spaces, we each behave differently, behaviors that get outwardly recorded and recognized as personality. Underneath these behaviors are certain beliefs acquired from experience. These beliefs can also lead to attitudes that may shift with time and experience. Underlying all of this, however, are the values that hold us up and speak to how we see ourselves.[6] Two types of values drive our thoughts, feelings and actions:

Instrumental values include values like collaboration, and achievement, things that we do with other people and that can confer a sense of belonging. These values power the ways that we live in the world.

Core values include things like love, justice, mercy. They serve as foundations for instrumental values and help us build a sense of purpose and belonging in the world.[7]

Instrumental values can change based on the stage of life, type of work one is doing and generally, the environment that we find ourselves in. A young person who places value on ascending the proverbial career ladder may, with the passing of time, switch and place a higher value on family, all while being the same person.

Core values on the other hand are stable over time and seasons. When we become attuned to our core values, we are able to shift our beliefs and our instrumental values, which can help us foster a more positive and engaged approach to relationships. These Core values are what we need to engage as we work on bringing back the 'be' in belonging.

Why Do We Need to Clarify Values for Belonging?

When we are in places where we know we belong, we are going to be enthusiastic (translated as a positive attitude). To see our enthusiasm (and love) reciprocated as a function of collective belonging, builds the belief that people are worth trusting. At work, it builds the belief that people in teams are worthy and capable of productive collaboration. These kinds of positive

THE BELONGING PARADOX

beliefs quickly become self-fulfilling with regards to belonging and belonging experiences.

Values clarification is therefore integral to knowing when our state belonging is being affected. If we clarified love and belonging as core subjective values, we will be readily aware of environments where these are not offered in meaningful ways. Same for fairness and justice. If we continue to stay in places where these values are violated, it can impact our belonging states. We need to know when a lack of belonging is due to misalignment of values. Being attuned to the match between our core values and our environments can help us work toward better present and future alignment. This work may include a physical or mental move to places that value us and what we have to offer.

•••••

The values clarification exercise I encourage here provides more than just a singular objective of avoiding misalignments with our environment. A secondary, and helpful objective is that once we are clear on our values, we will not spend precious time attempting to convince others about things they do not value. Remember, subjective values are called so for a reason.

What about you?

Do you know your core values?
Can you relate your core values to attempts at fostering belonging for others?

William R. Miller, the co-founder of Motivational Interviewing has a values clarification exercise available for public use.[a] The VIA institute on Character hosts the VIA (formerly Values in Action) strengths survey for identifying top character strengths.[b]

From Miller's work, I sorted ten core values: kindness, honesty, truthfulness, loyalty, intelligence, wisdom, openness, adventurousness, thoughtfulness, and courage. For the VIA character survey, my top strengths include curiosity, a love of learning, honesty, spirituality, fairness, bravery, and kindness, (in no particular order). Acknowledging these values help center me because in situations when I am afraid to speak up, I remember, as one example, that bravery is a core value for me. This allows me muster the courage I need to speak without fear. When it comes to enhancing belonging for others, the values I embrace to ensure that all voices are heard include curiosity, kindness and fairness.

While many of these strengths assessments provide results based on responses to objective and subjective values, remember that the people around us can also observe whether our behaviors are congruent with any professed values.

---

[a] Personal Values Card Sort:
https://www.guilford.com/add/miller11_old/pers_val.pdf?t=1
[b] Character Strengths, https://www.viacharacter.org/character-strengths-via

2. Fortify Your Self-concept

> *You are your best thing*
> —Toni Morrison

Some people, it appears, have naturally higher levels of confidence, exuberance, and extroversion, traits that make easing into new company easier for them than for others. If you happen to be an introvert or non-extrovert, you can fortify your self-concept and build up your inner and outer world by priming yourself to be more open to experience. Openness to experience is one of five dimensions that make up the continuum of the personality model known as the **Big 5** (for openness, conscientiousness, extroversion, agreeableness and neuroticism).[8] My focus on openness is deliberate. Increased openness to experience can enhance ability to engage without feeling threatened when we encounter new experiences or situations. Being more open to experience opens up our world, so that when we are in new places, with people who are different, we can participate and reflect on our experience where necessary without any preconceived notions or judgments.

3. Take The Belonging Mindset Outward

> *It is the individual who is not interested in his fellow men that provides the greatest injury to others.*
> —Alfred Adler

Psychologists talk about the concept of future goal-directed behavior; that we always work toward a future where we can have those things that are important to us. The Austrian psychologist, Alfred Adler, confirmed the socially embedded nature of human development, identifying the human tendency to act in ways we deem meaningful to our social environments. Adler also defined key areas (or life tasks) that humans need (or value) in order to make life more meaningful. He believed that work, friendship, and love or intimacy were the three basic life tasks needed for a meaningful life. Humans can fulfill these tasks through value-adding meaningful work, satisfying relationships with others, and love for oneself and others. Three additional tasks—recreational, spiritual, parenting (family)—have since been added to Adler's original theory.[9]

Through his work, Adler emphasized the importance of relationships and satisfying connections to others in our larger communities. The [belonging] stories in this book cut across five life areas— family, friendships, work, spiritual, and parenting—or spaces where we most seek and prize belonging. As occupants of social spaces, we are always trying to belong and fit into the fabric of the society. The goal for this final practice is to take the belonging practices listed earlier into future life spaces to enhance belonging for others. And we do this best when our initial family experiences combine to positively shape our worldviews.

How Can We Create Signals of Belonging for Others?

For those who may not have been raised in a stable and loving family, there can still be a focus and emphasis on social interests through practices that enhance collective belonging.

THE BELONGING PARADOX

We can focus on:

a) Increasing our levels of cooperation and participation in the common good through taking care of shared spaces and other communal activities that enfold multiple cultures. Think—participating in civic events, mentoring, tutoring, volunteering with and for others in shared community causes, hosting communal gatherings like potlucks and book or poetry readings and hobby clubs.
b) Practicing radical empathy and compassion for others in our life spaces. As we do this, we will beam signals of belonging out to others that mark us as people who desire only good for those in relationship with us.

★★★★★

In the **friendship** section, we learned how shared worldviews increase our friendship fitness and compatibility. We can learn to see others' worldviews through shared experiencing. We can enter into an empathetic experience of others' world views even if we do not share those views. We appreciate other people's views without a desire to change their views. We are able to do this because we know who we are at the core. We know those core values that enable us have an integrated sense of self. At **work and school**, we can practice small, wise interventions. These do not have to cost much but will offer huge rewards in terms of increasing belonging states for us and for others. As leaders, we can learn to practice procedural justice and fairness within all ethical boundaries. As **parents**, we can share in other parents' joy and angst, letting them know they are not alone. We can also practice being present for others. We can learn to practice the fine art of encouragement;

to inspire with hope, to give help and to spur on in the journey of living and parenting.

Adler, and many practitioners after him put forward a model of human growth and flourishing to remind us that our fates are never fixed or predetermined. The work of ensuring belonging is a reminder that we are always in the process of becoming. So, when we get discouraged due to difficult life interactions that impact our sense of belonging, we must remember that we can grow out of those states of discouragement. And as we grow, we should offer the same beacons of encouragement (and belonging) to others in our social worlds.

The TL;DR Version of The Belonging Practices.

1. THINK WELL (of yourself as a human created to belong).

2. SEE WELL (of yourself as a value-able person, worthy of belonging).

3. ACT WELL (use the thinking and seeing practices for others in your life).

THE BELONGING PARADOX

A CODA FOR BELONGING

To be is to exist
To long is to yearn
To be-long is to exist and to long for a place within or among.
Belonging to oneself is to find that place within that we occupy with the fullness of who we are; our strengths, foibles, follies and all, without self-judgment.
Belonging among is to take the fullness of that self into life spaces, recognizing that we have everything we need, whether others recognize it or not.

~ Author

Boundaried
Know your limits. Where and when to go to find belonging

Empathetic
Practice radical empathy toward yourself and others

Loose
Shake loose from attachment to outcomes

Oriented
Locate yourself in the right spaces, places and people

Needful
You are needed simply as you are. No questions asked.

Grace-filled
You don't have to pay to play in the fields of true belonging

A pocket card summary of The BELONG framework

Fostering Belonging at Work

Just because something is available instantly to vision does not mean that it is available instantly to consciousness.

—Jennifer Roberts (Art Historian)

In the preceding section, I presented what one might consider general belonging practices. But work for many adults is a valued and primary life task and many of us strive for meaningful work, seeing as we are likely to spend a majority of our lifetime working. As one who has had to straddle various work environments with different teams and leaders, I have found the workplace to be a big driver of belonging (or non-belonging) for many. In this next section, I put on my organizational psychologist hat and step into working definitions and practices for enhancing organizational belonging for self and others. As a woman born and raised to adulthood in one country, now living and working in another, I am aware that organizational practices are culture dependent. I write therefore, from a liminal space perspective, on contextual practices in two countries in two different worlds.

Organizational Belonging: Right and Not So Right Ways

An organization is both the administrative and functional structure of an entity and is also the humans who make up these structures.[a] Thinking of organizations in binary terms of profit or non-profit can take focus away from the people who are in them and set up environments that do not reflect belonging as a value in shared spaces. People are said to be **enculturated** into organizations when they conform to and comply with an organization's standards and requirements.[b,3] Standards in the form of policies and procedures put in place to make the administrative oversight of organizations more structured and less subject to diverse human interpretations. Yet, uneven enforcement of such standards by human leaders can cause undue hardship to the other humans working in organizations.

To speak of human belonging in a Western culture replete with transactional mindsets in the process and practice of work, will not be an easy conversation. The industrial revolution of the last century brought with it, speed and efficiency and the concept of maximizing human productivity. While efficiency of processes and productivity are good goals, humans are not work machines that are to be optimized for simple capital gains. The concept of maximizing human productivity is contradictory in both form and function.

---

[a] "organization". *Merriam-Webster.com*. 2024.
[b] "enculturation". *Merriam-Webster.com*. 2024.

THE BELONGING PARADOX

Talk about the industrial revolution is not nostalgia for the good old times or the way that things were. Because while industrial changes improved standards of living, it also brought with it what I call a separation of 'human, church, and state'. The human communities that helped people belong and find value and meaning to life, were slowly separated by the culture of individualism (a state).

With more work and educational activities increasingly being carried out in teams and team-based environments, comes a crucial need to examine practices that help (or hinder) peoples' sense of work belonging. My goal here is to offer practices that can be used by leaders and members within various organizations to increase belonging in the workplace.

Work and Belonging: Goals from Survey Results

This would not be the first (or the last) book to talk about the importance of fostering a sense of belonging in the workplace. A representative national survey on belonging in the US reported widespread feelings of non-belonging across all aspects of American life.[1] Of those who responded, sixty four percent reported non-belonging either in terms of belonging uncertainty or in actual exclusion in the workplace. In this survey, the Americans, in contrast, reportedly experiencing belonging, were healthier, had increased job and work satisfaction, increased trust in others and in the government, and increased civic engagement.

Other reports and studies have shown that an increased sense of belonging at work can give rise to increased employee engagement and what is known as organizational citizenship behaviors or OCBs.[2,3] These behaviors include tasks and projects that employees take on without being asked to, sometimes leading to extra working time spent on their own accord.[4] While time spent at work may indeed be a measure of productivity (there is that word again), I do not consider it a true metric for organizational citizenship behavior. Rather, organizational citizenship consists of things like altruism, courtesy to others, civic engagement and being in tune with how the organization works.[5] Additionally, I consider individual learning and knowledge sharing with others as part of these discretionary actions. In this sense, fostering organizational belonging can be both a corporate and an individual goal.[6]

At the corporate level, understanding the basis of what ensures belonging for the various people within the organization is a key step in creating a culture of workplace belonging for all. Today, we have more than a fair share of data and information available from studies and research on belonging from surveys and demographics-based reports like the Belonging Barometer.[1]

At the individual level, understanding belonging uncertainty and how to reframe the ways in which we perceive differences in others' behaviors and cultures is an important skill. Practicing these skills may lead one to increase their participation and engagement in work-related extracurricular activities, which paradoxically can enhance feelings of workplace belonging.

For the People, By the People

No matter the practices highlighted in this book, belonging will always come down to the human experience. Even when

THE BELONGING PARADOX

organizations lack the resources to care for the people in them, as dealt with frequently in countries like my birth country, it was (and still is) the people that made belonging at work a way of life. The human care and belonging we found at work was one of the people, by the people. If one was down in the manner of the troubles that sometimes befell people living without adequate social nets, it was people who came to your aid. It was people who entered your story through thinking and caring about you as a human being at work.

Becoming Wise About Belonging: To Care is to Intervene

A lack of and eventual satisfaction of basic human needs like food, water or shelter, is easy to measure and to quantify. As key as belonging is to human flourishing, logical problem-solving techniques may not readily apply to the issue of workplace belonging. One might even call workplace belonging a wicked problem (to stretch this term), because its psychological and emotional roots tend to complicate the determination of an endpoint where everyone's needs are met.[7] Not everyone places the same values on interventions for increased belonging. Practices that work for some in terms of belonging needs may make no difference to others. Similar to other human motivations, what people expect for fulfillment of their expressed needs (whether actual or perceived) can impact the effectiveness of any organization-wide interventions designed to foster work belonging.

Many companies promote identity-based employee resource groups as practical interventions for belonging. While these affinity and identity groups are one way to help employees develop positive feelings about their multiple social identities, using them as a presupposed panacea for increased belonging can backfire. There are documented issues with people over-identifying with social groups. One consequence of such over-identification is a further perpetuation of in-group and out-group dynamics and associated intergroup conflict.[8]

THE BELONGING PARADOX

I have come to think that some of the low priority placed on belonging at work comes from the highly distinct boundaries between work and life that prevail in individualistic (and highly litigious) societies as seen with the US. When people are socialized to separate aspects of their lives in this manner, it can lead to a dehumanization of the very human side of people working with each other, similar to what obtains in negative intergroup relations.[9] This demarcation can also feed into a "They're not like us" mindset toward people from different demographics. As a result, to avoid any missteps and corresponding liability, people may not want or care to know more about individuals from other groups, this being one of the first steps to seeing them as persons worthy of belonging.

This group boundary distinction is observed within hierarchical work cadres; administration versus non-administration, superintendent/faculty/staff, managers/non-managers, teacher/student, you name it. Any work groups with boundaries in which only shallow contact exists can foster non-belonging. Especially if those boundary lines are consistently flaunted by members in the dominant power category. Obvious here will be the fact that many of the groupings I describe have nothing to do with racial or ethnic majorities in the sense that we know it. Because in recalling the apartheid system of government in South Africa with its inhumane system of work and life segregation, the ethnic Dutch minority were actually the dominant (power) majority.

♦♦♦♦♦

Not every business has or needs to have diverse and multicultural teams. I am not trying to make the case that every organization must become diverse in all of the ways we understand diversity. After all there are niches for women-, minority-, veteran-, Native American- and other identity centric businesses in the US (and other parts of the world).[10] Having said that, even where a business does not need a diverse team, it still carries out its enterprise in a diverse, multicultural ecosystem, which also calls for cross-cultural intelligence.

This section focuses on practices for organizations and business units composed of multicultural employees who carry out the company's mission from a local and global perspective. In healthcare and higher education, two fields I worked in, while the presence of multicultural workers was a given, I came to see that being surrounded by such diversity did not mean coworkers and leaders practiced and reflected workplace belonging. In some of these organizations I witnessed practices that were based on the culture allowed by the leader of a subunit, and not typical of the larger organization. For any leader of a group or team therefore, one implicit marker of their success as leaders is to ensure belonging for all members of the team.

THE BELONGING PARADOX

Ways to Enhance Organizational Belonging

🌐 Create a Culture and Practice of Cultural Intelligence

As a leader, knowing what you don't know and being willing to admit it takes a lot of humility and vulnerability. To build belonging for people at work —many of whom will be from different cultural backgrounds whether of family, regional township or national—will require humility. A culturally focused humility that does not presume that only leaders know what fosters a sense of belonging at work. The knowledge of different belonging rituals and practices and how these are perceived by different groups is essential if we want to take a multicultural approach to enabling belonging. Leaders need to move away from the one size fits all approach to belonging practices. Practices to enable belonging should be considered like other human motivations involving rewards where different people are motivated by different ideals. As an example, if an organization provides food for employees as perks, are foods from different parts of the world normalized as lunch offerings? Are there opportunities for wholesome stories of such foods, stories told either by leaders or employees (see storytelling practice). Do leaders come down to eat with employees even if for brief periods?

☼ *Offering different types of belonging practices can ensure that people will find one or more that makes them feel welcomed in place.*

⑧ Cue for Environmental Belonging

People can come to different conclusions based on the same event or situation. This ability to make meaning also applies to belonging and belonging needs. Environmental cues like those popular "You Belong Here" signs may not have the same psychological impact on everyone in the environment. In fact, some studies suggest that displaying signs like these can actually lower signals of belonging for certain groups. In a study on belonging in college students, sending college swag to new students did not increase a sense of affiliation and belonging among Black students compared to their white counterparts. For the Black students, the issues on their minds related to stereotyping and social identity threat; the possibility of people attributing negative group level attributes to them as individuals. These students were more concerned about being respected and valued at school than with identifying with the new institution based on external markers like apparel.[4] The same concept goes for work. Giving out company swag, while laudable and appreciated by employees, is not likely to satisfy belonging needs for all groups.

To use this practice, Leaders need to ask, "Where and how do the different questions of belonging arise in teams or organizations?" and then provide signals and environmental cues that show that diversity of thought, expression, from people at work is welcomed. Such cues should be prominently displayed and rotated through as needed. This is not a call to only use the same themed identities in corporate communications and messaging. The goal is to show that everyone is welcomed and not to highlight certain social groups.

THE BELONGING PARADOX

☼ *People can and will draw meaning from various cues in the work environment. Leaders can use this knowledge to diversify symbolic cues.*

Encourage a Dynamic, Flexible Growth Mindset Around Mistakes and Learning Ability

This is especially crucial for enabling newer hires in organizations. Anyone who has ever began work or life in a new social environment may recall how much work it was to observe social cues around work practices and behaviors and to learn from these.

Leaders who are mindful of this will reinforce the organization's value through learning simulations and real-life modeling of accountability and work ethics. This way they signal to new employees that belonging in the workplace will not be impacted by on-the-job learning curves, no matter how steep that curve may be for some.[11] Members and leaders of organizations have a responsibility to help newcomers understand that ability is not fixed and can be further developed as they learn on the job. This means creating the necessary runway for such learning and not expecting them to "hit the ground running" as is the custom in many resource-scarce units. The feeling of being left alone to figure things out, right after new hire orientations, can contribute to a loss of confidence and lowered state belonging. Outcomes that no good manager would ever want for their new hires.

☼ *Leaders who create space for adequate on-the-job learning and who have a growth mindset around mistakes help foster belonging at work.*

📖 Tell Belonging Stories and Allow Reciprocity

Stories are how we make sense of the world. Leaders need to create room for belonging stories especially from people at various stages of tenure within the organization (see new hire learning curve in practice 3) Many of our individual life and work stories will include experiences of failures and successes. Telling these stories from a place of safety allows others to see people in different ways. The Afghan people, when speaking of shared experiences through story, say, "Someone entered my story," reflective of a sense of belonging in the presence of others.[12] Telling our stories of workplace belonging allows others to see that certain work experiences are encompassing.[11] It allows them enter our stories, and us theirs.

As an immigrant woman, who attended graduate school and had no one to serve as a model and guide for job searches, I am no longer ashamed to tell the story of how I flopped my very first interview. It took a dear friend who was working full-time and going to graduate school to point me in the right direction as to what I should have done. Obviously, I did not get the job. This unsuccessful outcome could have been due to multiple reasons, but it was hard to detangle associating this outcome from my profound lack of awareness about interviewing protocols.

I tell this story to clients and students to say, I too once had a major faux pas in my job searching experience and they are welcome to learn from my mistakes. I have been told that this story speaks to my ability to keep it real. I do not know about this. I only know about my desire to make it easier for immigrants and others in liminal spaces in their career. My story is a reminder that one mistake will not be the end, especially for those who did not have anyone like my friend to show them the hidden curriculum —those ways of being that can assure success, the ones that people in inner circles know but the rest of the room do not know—of surviving and thriving in a new country.

☼ *As a member-leader, creating opportunities for work stories of entry into the workforce can foster belonging, especially for newer team members.*

Create Opportunities for Positive Contact Among All Employees

Work in intergroup relations has shown that due to social identity, people will segregate into groups with people who are most like them.[9] This is not necessarily a bad thing because our social identities can give us a measure of our place in the world. The trouble arises in a multicultural and pluralistic society like the US where various groups have to spend significant amounts of time together at work. People in the workplace (or in teams) can react negatively, albeit unconsciously, to the presence of others who are different from them. They may be reacting to symbolic threats, due to perceived differences in morals, values and standards between them and members of another group. Some may also carry the burden of intergroup anxiety (toward people in a particular group) from personal anxiety based on actual or anticipated interactions with members that group.[9]

If you think these are all in people's minds, and therefore contrived, try telling that to my friend, Sati, who told me about the time a white woman told her that she felt nervous about her husband having Black male friends, because her first fiancé was killed by a Black man. Sati, a Black woman, had to sit and listen to this confession, because she was considered a safe friend. Did you smile or shake your head in astonishment at the irony? People's anxieties are real to them even if based on unfounded fears. Imagine someone with such anxiety being on a team with a Black man at work. Rudimentary training videos about implicit bias will not be enough to assuage their internalized fear or anxiety.

Enter the positive contact idea for building bridges between dissimilar groups.[28] This practice speaks to having greater intentionality around those ubiquitous team building activities. Leaders must go beyond their comfort zones to create or facilitate cooperative interpersonal experiences to enable positive contact between different groups of people (similar to a benign form of exposure therapy). The cooperative aspect of positive contact is key because competition can breed further hostility.

To enable positive contact in team building experiences and activities, certain conditions are necessary—

    a. There should be visible support from the organization's leadership.
    b. Social norms highlighting the importance of these activities to organizational mission and goals should be created.
    c. The activity should promote interdependence with everyone contributing equally to the solution.
    d. Everyone should have equal status during the activity time, no matter who they are.

I can think of activities that meet many of these conditions like when teams come together for social projects such as building houses for Habitat for Humanity. Seeing everyone at work putting together a house for a family in need can lead to a heightened sense of belonging at work. While making the time to build houses may not be feasible for all teams, leaders (and team members) can think of activities that promote many of the conditions for positive intergroup contact and go ahead and try them out.

Increase opportunities for members from different groups at work to come together in a cooperative atmosphere.

🏆 Reward Positive Belonging Norms

Humans are social creatures, subject to formal and informal persuasion modes. When leaders create room for telling belonging stories (see practice 4) through mixed media, or create a culture of recognition (see practice 1) that highlights employees who help create a sense of belonging for others at work, people notice. Recognition is like a balm for many workers. Adding the ability to enhance belonging for others as a positive celebrated organizational norm can create a virtuous cycle with employees looking for ways to add to the organization's belonging story bank. This virtuous loop can happen because humans want to be thought of as people who do the right things, even if those right things are built on workplace derived norms.

Helping others belong is a right thing to do, even when others do not notice. But bringing this right thing into the public arena for recognition can serve the function of elevating belonging for other people. Now someone might protest that this can be used in Machiavellian ways for gaining political clout or status. And while this may be true for some people, the principle of a rising tide lifting all boats will still apply. If everyone in an organization followed a culture of creating belonging, there will be no need for anyone to take undue advantage simply for rewards.

☼ *Promote meaningful visible rewards for individuals who create a positive belonging atmosphere for others at work.*

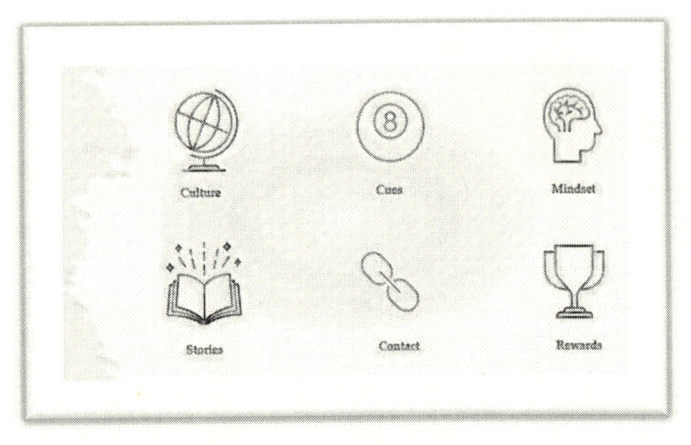

Six Ways to Embed Belonging at Work

Thinking Beyond Six Practices

There are many other small but highly significant ways to foster belonging for others at work. Things that do not require a budget but still can add to employees' sense of belonging at work. Small acts, thoughts and words of care for employees need not be a cost item. In the section on work belonging stories, I wrote about not receiving any form of encouragement from my supervisors for a very long time. No matter how I try to spin it, in the aftermath, I cannot hold this up as an exemplary case of care from a leader. In a case of

THE BELONGING PARADOX

modeling what I desired, I did not let my leaders' actions prevent me from entering into the stories of my own team of students, to see them and encourage them through what was undoubtedly a scary time for all of us at the time.

While many of these practices seem accessible and can be checked off as organizational inclusion goals, belonging interventions can lose steam and become ineffective. This happens when practices aimed at fostering belonging appear inauthentic or coercive, or when people fail to connect such exercises to their broader personal experiences. Using the example of the house building team experience, having employees who are not paid enough to afford secure housing can come across as employer grandstanding if pictures of such activities are used in corporate communications to highlight team building successes.

Organizational belonging is not limited only to the symbolic meanings that employees draw from belonging practices but also includes lived realities and access to tangible resources at work. When leaders do everything to increase belonging for individuals or groups at work and yet those team members cannot pursue career actualization goals due to resource or structural barriers, then there's a bigger problem at hand. Therefore, efforts to increase belonging will also need to address systemic barriers— hiring, unequal practices around performance evaluations and promotions, positional visibility and success— for all persons within the organization.[11] Doing the work to dismantle some of these entrenched work practices and assuring people of organizational and procedural justice will go much further in reflecting belonging at work for all rank and file employees than any activity or event or infrequent bonus payments will ever do.

Concluding Thoughts

I wrote this book using what I called an **_em-etic_** approach — a mashup word created by combining the terms "emic" and "etic," two anthropological approaches to studying human cultures.[1] In an 'etic' approach, one observes a culture neutrally and describes it without any prior assumptions. In the 'emic' approach, one lives within the culture and tries to explain what they observe as an insider. As an immigrant woman, I approached observations on certain aspects of culture and living life in the US with an 'etic' lens. But I put on an 'emic' hat in my observing and recounting belonging experiences while living here.

As a pharmacist, I cannot help but bring another perspective to the use of an emetic approach in sifting through belonging experiences. In medicine, an emetic is a drug used to induce vomiting.[2] While we might think of vomiting as nauseating, sometimes there will be an urgent need to rid the body of noxious elements that were (intentionally or unintentionally) ingested. In such a sense, then, using an emetic is good for the body. Taking an emetic brings needed alignment to the poisoned body, so that it is better able to take in good, healthy and nourishing substances. From this perspective then, (as a medicine woman), I hope for three things for readers through this book:

1. That you are able to get rid of noxious beliefs around belonging and what you need to do to fit in and belong. And when done, that you share with others, as part of practicing belonging and including others in our world (and worldviews).

THE BELONGING PARADOX

2. That as you begin the journey back to self and others using The BELONG framework, that your world, like that of a generous person, gets larger and larger.
3. That as you continuously learn to belong to yourself, that you find the ultimate belonging paradox, the fine art of belonging —according to Maya Angelou— "nowhere and everywhere."[3]

You will pay a price (for being free), but it will be worthwhile.

From my traveler's heart to yours.

Otito Iwuchukwu

Acknowledgments

How does one measure individual contributions to a work like this? My attempts at thanking various people here should not be taken as a slight to anyone not featured in what I consider as paltry a list as I can make with my limited powers of remembrance.

If I were to count each and every one who added to my life and therefore to this book reaching its readers, a thousand words (and tongues) would not do.

I want to thank my wonderful partner, @StanleeO, for holding the forte while I wrote this book. My journey to belonging would not be complete without him as faithful companion through the wild turns and rides over the years.

I owe a debt of gratitude to the many individuals featured in the belonging stories, because without these experiences, good (or bad), I would not have any stories to tell and to learn from.

To my dad and (late) mom, the ones under whose roof I learned what family was all about. Again, without you both, my story would never have begun all those decades ago. I may not show it all the time but I am thankful to be the last-born in your family. And to my siblings, thank you for the richness of our sibling group dynamics. I love us so much and would not exchange us for any other.

To all those I call my friends (and who call me friend too)—every single one of you makes life so much more meaningful. From Unibadan family of friends, to friends made in graduate and postgraduate school, and to new friends made in the social hub for Black female pharmacists, I am blessed to have met you all. To my close friend, Buks, the one I met 22 years ago in that wonderful open plan office at our first job right out of

Acknowledgements

school, thank you for making me a part of your family through our friendship, even when I said I would not do family friend attachments (I cannot say I truly succeeded at this because she has accused me of 'stealing' her sisters from her, and her sisters of stealing her close friend). To the many friends whose positive belonging stories I carry in my heart, you know who and where in the world you are; in Pennsylvania, California, Georgia, New Jersey, Calgary, London, New Zealand... what a blessing to be in your friendship circles. To my mommy group friends, being a part of your friendship posse has been a bounty of Black and beautiful goodness. To my Black Ivory and Azusa groups, our prayers and chats served to sustain me through academia. What a ride we have all had as women navigating this peculiar life space.

Lastly no book is ever self-written or published. There is a small army of people holding up the hands of the author through the many (some of them painful) steps that must be followed in order for a published work to make it to market. I want to specially thank the three doctors who reviewed my writing and offered honest and loving critiques—the care and labor of love you put into it made the many drafts before editing so much better.

Any omission of the many wonderful and amazing humans in my life is not deliberate. For these individuals, I would add my last thank you.

Postscript

This book almost did not belong. Yes, the book you are reading, almost did not make it out of my head and into you, the reader's hands. I almost did not write this book, because I was afraid. And yet here you are holding this book that was almost not written. But this fear I speak of is one that I have learned to come to terms with. A fear that author, Meera Lee Patel —to speak of paradoxical things—calls "friend."*

While motivational speakers (and writers) tell me to "Feel the fear and do it anyway", I was raised on scriptural imperatives to "Fear not" and to "Not be afraid." Each time (everyday) I faced emotionally debilitating fear I would think, "Am I not believing enough for the imperatives to be apparent in my heart and in my life?" But then I am reminded of the story of Joshua, Moses's successor. The directive to him was to: "Be strong and courageous" (Joshua 1:8, NJKV). These are surely not words spoken to a person who is already strong and brave.

This to me, means we can be both fearful and brave. To be courageous in the face of fear is synonymous with doing, with acting in pursuit of goals. This paradox of courageous fear is the singular reason you are holding this book right now.

A question for you: What courageous thing ~~can~~ will you do in the face of fear?

Go. Do it!

---

*Patel Meera Lee 2018 *My Friend Fear: Finding Magic in the Unknown*

Bookending Family Belonging: A Story and a Poem

I have known JJ for over 7 years. She is my Saturday morning walking companion. She is so wise and resourceful and I consider her a force to be reckoned with (which says a lot). I always knew she was a middle child with something she would constantly refer to as "middle child syndrome." When I asked her to share her belonging story, she sent me the story you will read here. I was enthralled to learn all these new things about her. Her story reminded me that we can outlive many big (and small) things that want to claim residence and live inside and outside our minds. I told JJ she needed to write her own book, but she insisted on sharing her story in mine. So, as part of the practice of belonging I write about, I am sharing my friend JJ's story, with you. Her Bert, as she calls him, is a wonderful man with a heart as big and tall as he is. I count myself blessed to have JJ in my friendship circle. I hope her story inspires you as much as it did me.

Belonging in Family: Through the Eyes of a Middle Child.

My older sister and I are exactly a year apart. I remember playing with her like sisters do. We did everything together. Our parents dressed us like Ernie and Bert from Sesame Street. I had a round face, and my sister had a long oval face. Personality-wise, she was slightly aloof while I would ask the hard questions and always try to figure things out. We were just perfect as our little family of four. My mom worked tirelessly and took care of the home while my dad, who also worked, preferred his weekends of leisure. Saturday mornings he would go play soccer with the league until 2 PM when he would return home for lunch. After lunch, he would spend the afternoons watching soccer on Telemundo. One of my first memories was waking up from a sound sleep hearing "GOAAALL" as he cheered when his team scored a goal. We were with him in the living room, but he wasn't really watching us; we were just in a room with another adult while my mom went grocery shopping, put everything away, began to prepare dinner, did laundry, ironed her uniform for the week, and washed and set her hair. Time was short for her, and her days often began before 6 AM to get our household in good shape for the week. She began by quietly cleaning the kitchen, bathrooms, and bedrooms. We would wake up to the smell of Pine-Sol, Ivory soap, and vinegar. She would then begin vacuuming after my dad left in the morning so she wouldn't disturb his sleep. While dinner was cooking and after she had done her hair, it was time for her to wash and plait our hair for the week. She worked quickly to make sure she was done by 6 PM because that was dinner time. My dad wanted his dinner served hot and on time. After dinner, my dad would return to the living room where he either had friends over watching sports or he would watch the news and sports entertainment channels until he retired to bed. After dinner, mom would take some time to teach us letters, numbers, colors, shapes, and how to read. I remember always falling asleep and waking up it seemed, with her always awake and wondering if she ever slept.

  One day, my auntie came to stay with us for a few days. Our parents were not home; in fact, I didn't know where they went. They had never left us before. My mom went to the hospital for the first time. My sister and I were born at home via midwife. They could not have gone on vacation, right?

THE BELONGING PARADOX

Vacations were things other people did, and the only time we traveled was back to my home country to fulfill obligations of food, money, service, and anything else people from the old country needed. We traveled with one or two outfits we wore for two weeks, and our luggage allowances were used to bring clothing, toiletries, medications, and anything requested by relatives.

Mom and Dad returned after a few days with a package. Wrapped in a little pink blanket was a baby. Where did this baby come from? Whose baby was this? When was the baby going back? As they took the time to explain, this was my new baby sister. I was adamant in saying I didn't want a baby sister at all. At that moment, I felt something shift even though I didn't know what it was at the time, but I know how it felt. Our family of four was forever changed. The attention I got as the baby was forever gone. My sister, on the other hand, was excited about having a new member of the household. She exclaimed, "That's my baby, my new baby sister!" She went to school and would come home with pictures she drew of the baby, art projects she made for the baby, etc. I just stared at the baby, who also just stared back, doing nothing but taking up space. My even number of two kids was now upset with a third wheel. The funny thing was the new "baby" it turned out was not the third wheel at all—I was.

As the now middle child, I grew up to become the sandwich child. Older sister was the one who got first dibs on everything—riding the bus, getting her first bike. And I got the obsolete hand-me-downs from all of it. Everything I wore it seemed was a leftover from my sister. Although times were lean, and money was tight, children only see what is in sight and not the circumstances that lend themselves to creating their reality. My baby sister was precious. She was adorned in new clothing, pink and precious. She received gifts from a baby shower thrown for my mom by her coworkers. A stroller, a highchair, pink dresses, ribbons, and new toys filled a closet.

I became resentful, always pointing out the situations where I felt I was being treated unfairly. I always had to "share" with my older sister. The baby never had to share. In fact, "my" sister, the older one, was now becoming best friends with the baby. She went everywhere with the baby. She was allowed to push the stroller, feed the baby, dress the baby, teach the baby, and play with the baby. I was sent to play outside because I was always "too young." I resigned myself to the fact that I had I lost my Bert. Ernie was now in a studio apartment alone.

As we grew up, older sister and I went to the same schools for many years. I tried get my "Bert" back until she became annoyed and told me, "Why can't you have your own friends? Why are you always hanging out with me?" I on the other hand admired her, wanted to learn from her and just be in her space. But she was growing too. She wanted to be alone with her own friends. She didn't want to share friends with me. She wanted to forge her own path and was tired of a little sister always hanging around.

After many years, by the time I was 14, I got the message. She was in high school now, and I was to keep my distance. I was the year behind and would be in high school soon, so I made a plan. I decided to break away and create the life I wanted. At the age of 14, I got a job; yes, someone was willing to hire me. I opened up a bank account, and I was finally able to afford a pair of jeans I had wanted, but the family budget would not allow. I always had money. Several days out of the week, I was able to afford a slice of pizza after school with a soda, which I would eat alone after school. It was something I enjoyed doing, and I enjoyed every bite. This was something I

THE BELONGING PARADOX

knew my family didn't do because the money was never there. My older sister would ask my parents for money so she could do the same. They denied her request for a time, but after about six months of this, they decided to grant her an allowance so she could enjoy what I had. It started when my mom and she came home with a pair of jeans. Mom had actually purchased my sister a pair of jeans! I was hurt and livid all at once. This was the same pair of jeans I was denied, found a job, earned the money, and purchased, yet they were just giving it to her for no effort on her part whatsoever. I asked my parents why. They basically said it wasn't a good look to have the younger sister have more than the older sister. They gave her an allowance as well—all in the name of making things look fair to my sister and everyone else outwardly looking. At one point, my mom went and found my sister a job. She filled out the application for her, set her hours after school so she too would have an income like I did. After three weeks of working, my sister quietly quit because she didn't want to work; she was content with getting an allowance from my parents.

Whether intentional or not, my parents set a competition between us. As high school carried on, I took on extra academic courses, and by the end of sophomore year, I was told I could graduate early if I wanted. This was an achievement for me. Maybe graduating with my sister would finally make my parents see us as equals. Graduation came; she was given money to host a dinner party for her friends, and I was told I would get the same gift next year—the year I was really supposed to graduate. I thought I had finally caught up in life and was no longer the unseen sister. No longer "Bert's sister," I was my own person. But that was not the case.

My first graduation party was me buying myself pizza and a soda, eating it alone after school. As I stood in the pizzeria, savoring my slice, I felt a mix of emotions. I was proud of my achievements, yet the loneliness weighed heavily on me. The pizza, once a symbol of my independence, now tasted bittersweet. I longed for the recognition and celebration my sister received, but more than that, I longed for the sense of belonging that seemed to have slipped away from me.

The following year, my "real" graduation year came and went without much fanfare. My parents did not fulfill their promise of giving me a dinner party, instead buying some cupcakes - but it felt like an afterthought compared to my sister's. The guests were mostly family members and a few of my own friends. The disparity in our celebrations stung, but I tried to focus on the fact that I was now truly free to forge my own path.

My sister went off to college out of state, and I went to a local university determined to make the most of my opportunity. Without the shadow of my sister over me, I began to flourish. I joined clubs, made new friends, and excelled academically. The independence I had cultivated during high school served me well, and I found a sense of fulfillment in my own achievements.

Despite the distance between us, I still sought my sister's approval. I would call her occasionally, updating her on my life and achievements, hoping she would be proud of me. She listened politely but remained distant. Our conversations were superficial, and the bond I longed to rebuild seemed further out of reach.

During my sophomore year of college, our parents announced they were visiting my sister. They extended an invitation for me to join them, and I reluctantly agreed, hoping

THE BELONGING PARADOX

it might be an opportunity to reconnect. The visit was cordial but strained. My sister had built a life of her own, and I felt like an outsider in her world. We shared polite conversations, but the deep connection I yearned for was absent.

After returning to college, I decided to focus on myself and let go of the constant need for my sister's approval. I threw myself into my studies, securing internships, and making meaningful connections with people who valued me for who I was. I started to realize that my worth wasn't dependent on my sister's validation or the fairness of our parents' actions.

By then, my parents were divorced. As often happens, most of the money went to attorneys, and with the split households, there wasn't enough for college. I had to navigate the world of college finances on my own. My sister could have helped, but we were competitors. I asked questions, went to the library to learn about FAFSA, scholarships, and ways to finance college. One way or another, I was determined to go to college. I managed to fund my education with loans and some grants, graduating with tens of thousands of dollars in debt. But my degree was something no one could take from me, so I worked multiple jobs to pay off my loans and maintain good credit. My sister graduated debt-free and moved forward in life earlier than I did, which had been her goal all along.

Years passed, and I graduated from college with honors. I landed a great job and began building a life I was proud of. My relationship with my sister remained distant, but I had learned to accept it. I found solace in the friendships I had built and the accomplishments I had achieved on my own.

One day, I received a call from my sister. She sounded different—softer, more vulnerable. She confessed that she had always felt the pressure of being the eldest, the one who had to set the example. She admitted that she envied my independence and resilience. For the first time, we had an honest conversation about our feelings, our childhood, and the unspoken competition that had driven a wedge between us.

We weren't Ernie and Bert anymore, but we found a new dynamic that worked for us. We supported each other in our individual journeys, recognizing our strengths and appreciating our differences. Looking back, I realized that the experiences that had driven us apart had also shaped us into who we were. My journey of feeling like the outsider child had taught me resilience, independence, and self-worth. It had pushed me to create a life where I stood on my own, not in anyone's shadow. And in the end, it brought me back to a place where I could rebuild my bond with my sister on new, healthier terms.

As older sister and I entered our twenties, we embarked on our careers, met partners, and carried on with life. My first partner was Abbie, a Muslim man from Africa. We were together for several years, learning what it took to cultivate a successful relationship. His vision for our future involved me converting to Islam, working both inside and outside the home, and always walking two steps behind him. He worked when he wanted and would leave jobs after six months for better opportunities. His money was his money, and my money was his money. He expected me to cook, clean, and have his dinner and laundry done on schedule. His weekends were for leisure, while mine were for housekeeping, grocery shopping, cooking, and laundry, with the eventual expectation of raising children.

After several years, I realized I was engaged to a man much like my father. It wasn't entirely his fault; he was handsome and charismatic, and we appeared to work well together. But I wanted more for myself, and unlike my mother, I had options. Abbie was a reckless spender, so I saved money and planned to exit. Confident in my future, whether it included him or not, I broke off our engagement after two years. The final straw was when he bought a motorcycle with shared funds without consulting me. He purchased it with cash from our joint account because he didn't qualify for a loan due to poor credit and a spotty employment history.

I found an apartment I wanted to purchase, and applied for a mortgage. By the grace of God, my research, job history, good credit, and perseverance, I had a closing date. We terminated our lease two months before our breakup.

On the afternoon of my closing, I was excited. I went to the bank, got my cashier's check, and bought a special pen to sign my papers. I scheduled an appointment with the attorney to divide our shared assets at 2 p.m. that day. The breakup was amicable, and Abbie still hoped for another chance. But I had mentally left the relationship months before. As we divided our assets 50/50, I looked at him with a blank stare while he looked at me with hope. He signed the papers, we hugged, and he prepared to leave. I asked him to stay and support me one last time. He agreed, and we moved to another conference room at 3 p.m. for the closing.

As I signed the contracts and other documents, his new reality set in. I was moving to a new home, no longer renting. When it was time for me to hand over my check and get my keys, his bottom lip trembled. He finally saw the result of not being in a collaborative relationship. Up until that point, he thought he held all the cards. He didn't count on me to move methodically and with perseverance to reach my goal of a down payment. Whenever he spent money from our account without discussing it with me, I would take the same amount from my next paycheck and move it to my down payment account. When he thought he was spending our shared money, he was really only spending his own. The epiphany hit him, and as I left the office that day, we shared a final hug, ending years of a relationship that taught us more about ourselves and our needs than anything else.

I was free and moved on, furnishing my new apartment and creating my new life. I decided to focus on myself and the life I wanted. I wasn't looking for a relationship or friends. I was looking to work, travel, and enjoy my life from that point forward.

One day, while shopping in New York after work, I bumped into my friend Craig. Craig and I knew each other from high school through our football conference, and we often saw each other at games. With my birthday approaching, I was planning a small dinner party and decided to invite him. Craig mentioned that he usually met with friends to watch sports and other activities on that day, so he asked if he could bring a friend. I happily agreed, thinking the more, the merrier.

As the weekend approached, Craig called to inform me that he couldn't make it after all; he needed to help his grandparents with some home repairs. I assured him that I'd invite him to the next gathering.

On Saturday night, as my friends arrived, they greeted each other and enjoyed the music. We were playing cards and having a great time when the doorbell rang. I answered it and found a handsome, 6-foot-6 man standing there. Assuming he was a Jehovah's Witness, I told him I had already taken the classes and Bible studies and that I had friends over. He corrected me, explaining that he wasn't a Jehovah's Witness but Craig's friend.

THE BELONGING PARADOX

This guy had traveled 30 miles into the woods to come to a party he wasn't directly invited to and wasn't even sure he'd be welcomed at. I had assumed that since Craig wasn't coming, his friend wouldn't either. Surprised, I invited him in, and my friends watched him cautiously. He had a kind face and a soft voice. Noticing the outsider looks he was getting, I decided to show him around, introducing him to a few people and offering him a plate of food: beans and rice, brown stewed chicken, cabbage, and plantains.

After finishing his first plate, he shyly asked for seconds and then requested the recipe. Eventually, he asked for my number.

The following week, he picked me up for a movie. We stopped for a quick bite, and he pointed out all the specials on the menu. During our conversation, he shared that he was living with his parents, who didn't really encourage him to leave. Instead, he was saving money to eventually buy a home. In the meantime, he worked and lived as frugally as possible. I realized that he was just like me—focused on saving for future goals. He was disciplined with his diet and had clear plans for the future.

Our relationship blossomed. He, too, was a middle child, often overlooked as his family focused on the eldest and the youngest. He was kind, treated me well, and had a quiet strength. He wasn't intimidated by my accomplishments and never hesitated to spend money on us, always mindful of his budget but never selfish with his time or attention. He saw our relationship as a partnership, a chance to learn and work together towards shared goals. After a few years, we became engaged, got married, and started a family.

From the beginning, he established himself as a true partner, invested in our shared outcome. He didn't know everything but was always willing to listen, learn, and adapt as needed. He was flexible and generous with his time and energy. Today, we live a life of shared responsibility for our household. We invest in each other, belonging to each other in our own little family. We're no longer outsiders in someone else's world; we are each other's world.

His name, by the way, was Bert. I'm his Ernie, the short one with the round face, and he's my Bert, the tall one with the oblong face. He's the yin to my yang, and after twenty years together, we don't argue. I no longer feel out of place or like the odd person out. We have discussions and compromises, not arguments and selfishness. I encourage everyone not to settle after all said and done in my family of birth, I found my Bert and created a family where everyone belongs.

An Immigrant-Citizen's Belonging Poem

Written by a doctor who has no qualms about stating her real name. No pseudonyms allowed because "Poems (and poets) are meant to be read" she said. For anyone out there looking; for the permission to be yourself no matter what, for the permission to live a (pseudonym) free life, here's a poem for you.

I am a perpetual foreigner, a third culture kid, a mixed nationality, citizen of the world. Born in England to two foreigners.

My mother, Guyanese, with strong upper class English mannerisms.

My father, Nigerian, who had lived outside of Nigeria, for most of his formative years. He could speak English, French, German and Yoruba.

Foreigners give birth to a perpetual foreigner.
Raised in Western Nigeria, but not really as Yoruba.
We said good morning, not *Ekaaro*.
English was the first language of our home.
We said, "Hi mom, hi dad" and did not bow, curtsy, genuflect, kneel or prostrate.

Few if any of the traditions of the Yoruba culture were a way of life.

I grew up speaking English in a West Indian twang with clipped British overtones.

This brought scorn and teasing from playmates.
"Why do you talk like that?"
So, I tried my best (as kids do) to fit in with the playground lingo, and rules.
As I did, my mother corrected my English, to "proper" English.
And a weird dichotomy set in.
I spoke one way at school and another way at home.
I did not want to be teased.
I did not want my mother correcting my "bad English"
And on and on it went through high school and medical school.

I heard time and again, "well you're not REALLY Nigerian".
"But you're only half Nigerian...."
"Oyinbo"(that means "white person")
"Oyinbo dudu" (that means "Black 'white person'")

Not really Nigerian?
I wondered if they were right.
After medical school, I left Nigeria and went to England
Surely I was English, because I was born here...
(Ha!)
"Where are you from?" I got asked time and again.
"I was born in Leicester"
"But where are you really from? Where are you from originally?"

I thought I spoke "proper English", certainly I sounded like everyone else.

I lived with Guyanese relatives, they said I was from Nigeria.

But I'm Guyanese.

"You're Guyanese and you DON'T like *pepperpot*?!"

Apparently, I was not really Nigerian, not really Guyanese, and not really English.

Once again, I heard:

"Why do you talk like that?"

A perpetual foreigner.

Moving stateside was interesting.

Having been in England I figured the societies would be similar.

Having watched American shows from the time I was child, I figured I would fit in with no problem.

I could do an American accent, I thought.

The USA is a land of immigrants, I thought.

No one cares where I'm from, I thought.

I will finally be from a place: USA!

(Ha!)

I said loo, instead of restroom

I said boot, instead of trunk

I said petrol, instead of gas (actually I said pe-TROLL)

I said accelerator, instead of gas pedal

I said windscreen, instead of windshield

I said manual, instead of "stick shift"

I said torch, instead of flashlight

I said biscuit, instead of cookie

I said sweet, instead of candy

I said trousers, instead of pants

I said pants, instead of panties
I could not speak Americanese!
As soon as I open my mouth, people ask:
"Where are you from?"
"Why do you talk like that?"
A perpetual foreigner, that is who I am.

Apart from being a "perpetual foreigner" I am also an internal medicine doctor, a life coach, a best-selling author and an international speaker. I have managed to parlay these "perpetual foreigner" gifts and perspectives into a unique niche!

—Dr. A. Ezeokoli

Notes

The WHO, WHAT or WHERE SECTION

I. BELONGING IN FAMILIES

1. "Genetic determinism" *in APA Dictionary of Psychology* American Psychological Association (2018), accessed April 30, 2024, https://dictionary.apa.org/.
2. Baumeister, R. F., and Leary, M. R. "The Need to Belong: Desire for Interpersonal Attachments as a Fundamental Human Motivation." *Psychological Bulletin* 117, no. 3 (1995): 497-529. https://doi.org/10.1037/0033-2909.117.3.497
3. Allen, K, Gray D. L., Baumeister R. F., and M. R. Leary. "The Need to Belong: a Deep Dive into the Origins, Implications, and Future of a Foundational Construct." *Educational Psychology Review* 34, no. 2 (2022): 1133–1156.
4. Pardede, S, and V B Kovač. "Distinguishing the Need to Belong and Sense of Belongingness: The Relation between Need to Belong and Personal Appraisals under Two Different Belongingness-Conditions." *Eur J Investig Health Psychol Educ* 13, no. 2 (2023): 331-344.
5. Ekman, Paul. *Universal Face Expressions "Are Facial Expressions Universal?".* https://www.paulekman.com/resources/universal-facial-expressions/
6. Ekman, Paul. *Fake Smile or Genuine Smile,* accessed July 15, 2024. https://www.paulekman.com/blog/fake-smile-or-genuine-smile/.
7. Paul Ekman, PhD, *The Truth about the Lie to Me TV Series.* https://lietome.com/the-truth-about-lie-to-me/
8. Bernstein, M. J., Young, S. G., Brown, C. M., Sacco, D. F et al. "Adaptive Responses to Social Exclusion: Social Rejection Improves Detection of Real and Fake Smiles." *Psychological Science* 19, no.10 (2008): 981-983.
9. Pickett, C. L., Gardner, W. L., & Knowles, M. "Getting a Cue: The Need to Belong and Enhanced Sensitivity to Social Cues." *Personality and Social Psychology Bulletin* 30, no.9 (2004):1095-1107.

Notes

10. US Department of Health and Human Services. "Adverse Childhood Experience." *Headstart.gov.* https://eclkc.ohs.acf.hhs.gov/publication/trauma-adverse-childhood-experiences.
11. Cohen, Gregory L. *Belonging: The Science of Creating Connection and Bridging Divides.* W. W. Norton & Company, 2022.
12. Ryan, R. M., and Deci, E. L. "Multiple Identities within a Single Self: A Self-Determination Theory Perspective on Internalization within Contexts and Cultures." In *Handbook of Self and Identity*, eds: Leary M. R. and. Tangney, J. P Guilford Press, 2013.
13. Forsyth, Donelson R. "Introduction to Group Dynamics." In *Group Dynamics*, by Donelson R Forsyth, Belmont, CA: Wadsworth Cengage Learning (2014)
14. The London Standard.. "Young Black gymnast appears to be snubbed during medal ceremony in Ireland." Video,. September 25, 2023, Youtube, 49 sec., https://www.youtube.com/watch?v=XcJkuWOhFtM.
15. Psychology Today. *Bystander Effect.* accessed August 25, 2024. https://www.psychologytoday.com/us/basics/bystander-effect.
16. McAdams, Dan P.. "The Ag 5–7 Shift." In *Art and Science of Personality Development*, ed: Dan P McAdams, Guilford Press, 2015.

II. BELONGING IN FRIENDSHIPS

1. Forbes.com, 2015, "Thoughts on the Business of Life." https://www.forbes.com/quotes/2585/.
2. Abrams, Zara. "The Science of Why Friendships Keep Us Healthy". *Monitor on Psychology*, American Psychological Association. June 1, 2023. https://www.apa.org/monitor/2023/06/cover-story-science-friendship.
3. William, Kasley. "Reveal Your Social Health Style." in *The Art and Science of Connection: Why Social Health is the Missing Key to Living Longer, Healthier and Happier*, HarperCollins, 2024.
4. Dunbar, Robin, "The Social Brain Hypothesis." *Evol. Anthropol.* no 6 (1998), 178–190.
5. Dunbar, Robin. "Homophily and the Seven Pillars of Friendship." in *Friends: Understanding the Power of our Most Important Relationships*, Brown Little, 2021.

6. Harel, T. and Koslowsky, M. D, "Development and Validation of the Relational Behavior Interactions Scale for Couples." *Sci Rep* 14, 8086 (2024). https://doi.org/10.1038/s41598-024-58901-2

III. BELONGING AT WORK

1. Annie E. Casey Foundation. Creating a Sense of Belonging: Young People Identify Ways to Build Welcoming Environments. August 30, 2021. https://www.aecf.org/blog/creating-a-sense-of-belonging.
2. Clance, P.R., and S.A. Imes. "The impostor phenomenon in high achieving women: Dynamics and Therapeutic interventions." *Psychotherapy: Theory Research and Practice* 15, no. 3 (1978): 241-247.
3. Association for Psychological Science. "One and Done: Researchers Urge Testing Eyewitness Memory Only Once." November 3, 2021. www.psychologicalscience.org/news/releases/2021-nov-pspi-eyewitness-one-and-done.html.
4. The World Bank. "World Bank Country and Lending Groups." https://datahelpdesk.worldbank.org/knowledgebase/articles/906519.
5. Pew Research Center. "Religion in India: Tolerance and Segregation: Attitudes about Caste." pewresearch.org. June 29, 2021. www.pewresearch.org/religion/2021/06/29/attitudes-about-caste/.
6. Hochschild, Arlie. R. The Managed Heart: Commercialization of Human Feeling. University of California Press, 1983.
7. Kihlstrom, John, F. "Person-Situation Interaction." www.ocf.berkeley.edu., 2013, https://www.ocf.berkeley.edu/~jfkihlstrom/PxSInteraction.htm.
8. Deci, E. L, and R. M. Ryan., "The "What" and "Why" of Goal Pursuits: Human Needs and The Self-determination of Behavior." *Psychological Inquiry* 11, no.4 (2000): 227-268. https://doi.org/10.1207/S15327965PLI1104_01
9. Omadeke, Janice.. What's the Difference Between a Mentor and a Sponsor? October 20. 2021. Harvard Business Review, https://hbr.org/2021/10/whats-the-difference-between-a-mentor-and-a-sponsor

IV. BELONGING IN THE FAITH

1. World Council of Churches. "Nigeria, Africa." Accessed September 24, 2024, https://www.oikoumene.org/countries/nigeria
2. Great Nonprofits. n.d. Sophia's Heart Foundation, Inc. Accessed October 2024. https://greatnonprofits.org/org/sophias-heart-foundation-inc.
3. Encyclopaedia Britannica. "*Assimilation.*" October 30, 2024. https://www.britannica.com/topic/assimilation-society.
4. Powatomi.org. "The True Dark History of Thanksgiving." November 25, 2020. https://www.potawatomi.org/blog/2020/11/25/the-true-dark-history-of-thanksgiving/.
5. Roderique, Hadiya. "Black in the Ivory Tower: Why it's so hard for academics of colour to pursue their dream projects." January 30 (2020) 2022. https://thewalrus.ca/black-in-the-ivory-tower/.
6. Rowe, Sheila Wise. *Healing Racial Trauma: The Road to Resilience*. IVP Academic, 2020.
7. Little, Becky. "Key Steps That Led to End of Apartheid." August 22, (2020) 2023.. https://www.history.com/news/end-apartheid-steps.
8. Brewer, M.B. 2002. "The Psychology of Prejudice: Ingroup Love and Outgroup Hate?" Journal of Social Issues https://doi.org/10.1111/0022-4537.00126.
9. McPherson, Miller, Lynn Smith-Lovin, and Cook James M. 2001. "Birds of a Feather: Homophily in Social Networks." *Annual Review of Sociology* (27) 415–44.

V. BELONGING IN PARENTHOOD

1. Pyschology Today. *Masking.* https://www.psychologytoday.com/us/basics/masking.

vi. BELONGING: A BRIEF EXPLAINER, OR TWO

1. Augsburger, David. W., "Individuality, Individualism and Solidarity: A Theology of Humanness." in *Pastoral Counseling Across Cultures*, by David. W Augsburger, The Westminster Press, 1986.

2. Mangena, Fainos., "Hunhu/Ubuntu in the Traditional Thought of Southern Africa." Internet Encyclopedia of Philosophy. November 15, 2024. https://iep.utm.edu/hunhu-ubuntu-southern-african-thought/
3. Baumeister, R. F, and Leary, M. R., "The Need to Belong: Desire for Interpersonal Attachments as a Fundamental Human Motivation." *Psychological Bulletin* 117, no. 3, (1995): 497–529.
4. Walton, Gregory M, and Shannon Brady., "The Many Questions of Belonging." in *Handbook of Competence and Motivation: Theory and Application*, eds: C. S. Dweck, & D. S. Yeager, A. J. Elliot, Guilford Press, 2017.
5. Jacobsen, Eric. "What is Belonging?" in *Three Pieces of Glass: Why We Feel Lonely in a World by Screens*, by Eric O Jacobsen, Brazos Press, 2020.
6. Jacobsen, Eric. 2020. The Crisis of Belonging. July 13. https://christiansforsocialaction.org/resource/crisis-belonging/

vii. A WALK THROUGH THE PARADOX OF BELONGING

1. Palmer, Parker J., *Let Your Life speak: Listening for the Voice of Vocation*. Josey-Bass, 1999.
2. Augsburger,. Pastoral Counseling Across Cultures, The Westminster Press, 1986.
3. Rogers, Kara. "Cell Differentiation." January 2, 2025. Encyclopaedia Brittanica https://www.britannica.com/science/cell-differentiation.

THE HOW-TO SECTION

I. A FRAMEWORK OF LIVED BELONGING

1. Wilkerson, Isabel., *Caste: The Origins of Our Discontent*. Random House, 2020.
2. Givens, Terri., *Radical Empathy: Finding a Path to Bridging Racial Divides*, Press, 2021.
3. Center for Substance Abuse Treatment (US). 2014. "*Exhibit 1-5 Cultural Identification and Cultural Change Terminology* in Introduction to Cultural Competence." Improving Cultural Competence. Treatment

Improvement Protocol (TIP) Series, No. 59. Substance Abuse and Mental Health Services Administration. Rockville (MD). www.ncbi.nlm.nih.gov/books/NBK248431

4. Earley, Christopher, P & Ang Soon., *Cultural Intelligence: Individual Interactions Across Cultures*. Stanford Business Books, 2003.

II. BRINGING BELONGING BACK TO SELF AND OTHERS

1. Alan E. Fruzzetti.. "Dialectical Thinking,." *Cognitive and Behavioral Practice* 29, no.3 (2022): 567-570.
2. Thorne, Brian. 2007. "Person-Centered Therapy in *Dryden's Handbook of Individual Therapy*, ed: Windy Dryden, Sage Publications, 2007.
3. Duerzen, Emmy Van., "Existential Therapy." In *Dryden's Handbook of Individual Therapy*, ed: Windy Dryden, Sage Publications, 2007.
4. Parrett, Malcolm, and Julie Denham. 2007. "Gestalt Therapy." In *Dryden's Handbook of Individual Therapy*, ed: Windy Dryden, Sage Publications, 2007.
5. Miller, William R.. "Getting Clear on Your Values." In *On Second Thought*, Guilford Press, 2022.
6. Rokeach, Milton., *The Nature of Human Values*. Free Press, 1973.
7. Augsburger, David W. "Values, Worldviews and Pastoral Counseling: A Theology of Values." In *Pastoral Counseling Across Cultures*, Westminster Press, 1986.
8. McCrae, R. R, and John O. P. "An Introduction To The Five-Factor Model and Its Applications." *J Pers.* 60, no. 2, (1992) 175-215.
9. Carlson, J., and Englar-Carlson, J., *Adlerian Psychotherapy*. American Psychological Association, 2017.

III. FOSTERING BELONGING AT WORK

1. The Belonging Barometer: The State of Belonging in America (Revised Edition). Over Zero & The American Immigration Council, June 2024, www.americanimmigrationcouncil.org/sites/default/files/research/thebelongingbarometer_revisededition_june2024_1.pdf.
2. Perry, Elizabeth., "Here's how to build a sense of belonging in the workplace." May 11, 2021. https://www.betterup.com/blog/belonging

3. Center for Creative Leadership. "How to Build Belonging at Work". accessed November 2024. https://www.ccl.org/articles/leading-effectively-articles/create-better-culture-build-belonging-at-work/
4. Neelie Verlinden, Gail Bailey. "Organizational Citizenship Behavior: Benefits and Best Practices." https://www.aihr.com/blog/organizational-citizenship-behavior/
5. Pickford, Helen Campbell, and Joy Genevieve. "Organisational Citizenship Behaviours: Definitions and Dimensions." August 30, 2016., Saïd Business School WP 2016-31,
6. Arruda, William.. "How To Cultivate a Culture of Belonging—And Why It's The Ultimate Competitive Edge." March 01, 2023. www.forbes.com/sites/williamarruda/2023/03/01/how-to-cultivate-a-culture-of-belonging-and-why-its-the-ultimate-competitive-edge/.
7. Interaction Design Foundation, IxDF "What are Wicked Problems?". June 4, 2016. https://www.interaction-design.org/literature/topics/wicked-problems.
8. Cikara, M. and Van Bavel, J. J. "The Neuroscience of Intergroup Relations." *Perspectives on Psychological Science* 9, no. 3 (2014): 245–274.
9. Brewer, Marilynn., "Intergroup Relations." *In Advanced Social Psychology*, eds: Roy Baumeister & Eli J. Finkel, Oxford University Press, 2010.
10. U.S. Small Business Administration. Business Guide. Accessed November 15, 2024. hhttps://www.sba.gov/business-guide/grow-your-business.
11. Walton, Gregory, and Mary Murphy. "15 Hacks for Building Diversity in Tech." Mindset Scholars Network. September 2015., http://gregorywalton-stanford.weebly.com/uploads/4/9/4/4/49448111/15_hacks_r1.1.pdf
12. Loewen, Arley. n.d. "Rethinking Shame and Honour." M-Series: Integral Foundations. im:press.

CONCLUDING THOUGHTS

1. Till Mostowlansky & Andrea Rota. "Emic and etic." The Open Encyclopedia of Anthropology, (2020) 2023., accessed November 22, 2024. https://www.anthroencyclopedia.com/entry/emic-and-etic

Notes

2. Encyclopaedia Britannica. "*emetic (drug)*." accessed November 22, 2024. https://www.britannica.com/science/emetic.
3. Bill Moyers: Original Series.. "A Conversation with Maya Angelou". November 21, 1973. accessed July 10, 2024. https://billmoyers.com/content/conversation-maya-angelou/

You can connect with Dr Otito Iwuchukwu through her website or through her social channels.

THE AUTHOR

OTITO F. IWUCHUKWU, PHD

- otitoiwuchukwu.com
- otitoiwuchukwu_phd
- @thebelonging.paradox
- /otitoiwuchukwu.authorpage

Made in the USA
Columbia, SC
15 June 2025